D0070149

"If someone wants to unleash the truth of people management, read this book. Author Robbins addresses the most critical challenges organizations face today in a concise and entertaining way."

— SUBIR CHOWDHURY
Executive Vice President, American Supplier Institute
Author of the best-selling The Power of Six Sigma *and*
The Talent Era: Achieving a High Return On Talent

"Stephen Robbins does it again! A prolific scholar and writer, he cuts through the research and theory to deliver immediately useful and essential insights for the effective management of people. I have never seen anything quite like *The Truth*. Excellent for all of us who don't take the time to keep up with leading edge thinking and practice in the field of management."

— ERIC G. STEPHAN, *Professor*
Organizational Leadership & Strategy
Marriott School of Management, Brigham Young University

"This is a clever book. Stephen Robbins has put together a book I wish I had written. It's a quick reference written for practicing managers, social scientists, and anyone interested in managing people. Robbins' 'best of' approach, as well as the reference materials each section draws on, make this book a 'must have' for practical, reliable, and valid information on the important leadership/management/people topics of the day."

— RANDALL P. WHITE, PH.D.
Principal, The Executive Development Group LLC
Co-author, Relax, It's Only Uncertainty

"The wide gap between management practice and behavioral research has finally been bridged. Steve Robbins' book translates what researchers currently know about managing people into clear and useful prescriptions for effective management. It should be the benchmark for anyone seeking advice on how to manage people."

— THOMAS G. CUMMINGS
Professor and Chair of the Department of Management and Organization
Marshall School of Business, University of Southern California

"Steve Robbins has truly pulled off what he said he would. Robbins has written a superb book that assembles evidence about some of the most useful information for managing people to achieve higher productivity and morale. Instead of belaboring and embellishing one concept throughout the book, Robbins presents the best evidence from many of the leading management researchers. The book is eminently practical, yet common sense is contradicted where it is proved to be wrong. In synthesizing the most useful information available on 63 key topics, Steve Robbins has made a substantial contribution to practicing managers. Researchers too should dig into this book to find out what is really known about managing people."

— ANDREW J. DUBRIN, PH.D.
Professor of Management and Industrial Psychologist
Rochester Institute of Technology

"What a service! The premiere writer of management textbooks has sifted through the research to extract the real nuggets—the (often-surprising) truths that every manager should know. This book is an antidote for the unsupported opinions handed out in many popular management books. Robbins lays out the rock-solid foundation for managing people—those central truths that are consistently supported by research. Ignore them at your peril!"

— KENNETH W. THOMAS
Professor of Management, Naval Postgraduate School, Monterey, California
author of Intrinsic Motivation at Work

"This is an important book for any manager, no matter the type of organization. Steve Robbins has combined two ingredients seldom found together in the typical business book: First, he speaks in language clearly understandable to managers. Second, he backs up his pithy discussions and conclusions by anchoring them in solid behavioral research findings. Definitely an interesting and highly informative read."

— LYMAN W. PORTER
University of California, Irvine

THE TRUTH

ABOUT MANAGING PEOPLE . . .
AND NOTHING BUT THE TRUTH

ISBN 0-13-066927-X

9 790130 669277   90000

FINANCIAL TIMES PRENTICE HALL BOOKS

For more information, please go to www.ft-ph.com

Thomas L. Barton, William G. Shenkir, and Paul L. Walker
Making Enterprise Risk Management Pay Off:
How Leading Companies Implement Risk Management

Deirdre Breakenridge
Cyberbranding: Brand Building in the Digital Economy

William C. Byham, Audrey B. Smith, and Matthew J. Paese
Grow Your Own Leaders: How to Identify, Develop, and Retain Leadership
Talent

Jonathan Cagan and Craig M. Vogel
Creating Breakthrough Products: Innovation from Product Planning
to Program Approval

Subir Chowdhury
The Talent Era: Achieving a High Return on Talent

Sherry Cooper
Ride the Wave: Taking Control in a Turbulent Financial Age

James W. Cortada
21st Century Business: Managing and Working
in the New Digital Economy

James W. Cortada
Making the Information Society: Experience, Consequences, and Possibilities

Aswath Damodaran
The Dark Side of Valuation: Valuing Old Tech, New Tech,
and New Economy Companies

Henry A. Davis and William W. Sihler
Financial Turnarounds: Preserving Enterprise Value

Sarvanan Devaraj and Rajiv Kohli
The IT Payoff: Measuring the Business Value
of Information Technology Investments

Nicholas D. Evans
Business Agility: Strategies for Gaining Competitive Advantage through Mobile Business Solutions

Kenneth R. Ferris and Barbara S. Pécherot Petitt
Valuation: Avoiding the Winner's Curse

David Gladstone and Laura Gladstone
Venture Capital Handbook: An Entrepreneur's Guide to Raising Venture Capital, Revised and Updated

David R. Henderson
The Joy of Freedom: An Economist's Odyssey

Philip Jenks and Stephen Eckett, Editors
The Global-Investor Book of Investing Rules: Invaluable Advice from 150 Master Investors

Thomas Kern, Mary Cecelia Lacity, and Leslie P. Willcocks
Netsourcing: Renting Business Applications and Services Over a Network

Frederick C. Militello, Jr., and Michael D. Schwalberg
Leverage Competencies: What Financial Executives Need to Lead

Dale Neef
E-procurement: From Strategy to Implementation

John R. Nofsinger
Investment Madness: How Psychology Affects Your Investing… And What to Do About It

Tom Osenton
Customer Share Marketing: How the World's Great Marketers Unlock Profits from Customer Loyalty

Stephen P. Robbins
The Truth About Managing People…And Nothing but the Truth

Jonathan Wight
Saving Adam Smith: A Tale of Wealth, Transformation, and Virtue

Yoram J. Wind and Vijay Mahajan, with Robert Gunther
Convergence Marketing: Strategies for Reaching the New Hybrid Consumer

FINANCIAL TIMES
Prentice Hall

In an increasingly competitive world, it is quality
of thinking that gives an edge—an idea that opens new
doors, a technique that solves a problem, or an insight
that simply helps make sense of it all.

We work with leading authors in the various arenas
of business and finance to bring cutting-edge thinking
and best learning practice to a global market.

It is our goal to create world-class print publications
and electronic products that give readers
knowledge and understanding which can then be
applied, whether studying or at work.

To find out more about our business
products, you can visit us at www.ft-ph.com

Pearson
Education

THE TRUTH
ABOUT MANAGING
PEOPLE ♦ ♦ ♦
AND NOTHING BUT
THE TRUTH

Stephen P. Robbins, Ph.D.

FINANCIAL TIMES
Prentice Hall

An Imprint of Pearson Education
London • New York • San Francisco • Toronto • Sydney
Tokyo • Singapore • Hong Kong • Cape Town • Madrid
Paris • Milan • Munich • Amsterdam

A CIP catalogue record for this book can be obtained from the Library of Congress.

Robbins, Stephen P.,
   The truth about managing people--and nothing but the truth / Stephen P. Robbins.
      p. cm. -- (Financial Times Prentice Hall books)
   Includes bibliographical references.
   ISBN 0-13-066927-X
      1. Supervision of employees. I. Title. II. Series.

   HF5549.12.R632 2002
658.3'02--dc21   2001058371

Production Editor and Compositor: *Vanessa Moore*
Acquisitions Editor: *Tim Moore*
Editorial Assistant: *Allyson Kloss*
Marketing Manager: *Bryan Gambrel*
Manufacturing Manager: *Maura Zaldivar*
Cover Design Director: *Jerry Votta*
Cover Design: *Talar Agasyan-Boorujy*
Art Director: *Gail Cocker-Bogusz*
Interior Design: *Tech Graphics*
Project Coordinator: *Anne R. Garcia*

© 2002 Prentice Hall PTR
Pearson Education, Inc.
Upper Saddle River, NJ 07458

Prentice Hall books are widely used by corporations and government agencies for training, marketing, and resale.

The publisher offers discounts on this book when ordered in bulk quantities. For more information, contact: Corporate Sales Department, Phone: 800-382-3419; Fax: 201-236-7141; E-mail: corpsales@prenhall.com; or write: Prentice Hall P T R, Corp. Sales Dept., One Lake Street, Upper Saddle River, NJ 07458.

All rights reserved. No part of this book may be reproduced, in any form or by any means, without permission in writing from the publisher. All trademarks mentioned herein are the properties of their respective owners.

Printed in the United States of America

10 9 8 7 6 5 4 3 2 1

ISBN 0-13-066927-X

Pearson Education LTD.
Pearson Education Australia PTY, Limited
Pearson Education Singapore, Pte. Ltd.
Pearson Education North Asia Ltd.
Pearson Education Canada, Ltd.
Pearson Educación de Mexico, S.A. de C.V.
Pearson Education—Japan
Pearson Education Malaysia, Pte. Ltd.

For my wife, Laura.

CONTENTS

Contents

PART III
THE TRUTH ABOUT LEADERSHIP
73

PART IV
THE TRUTH ABOUT COMMUNICATION
105

Contents

Contents

PREFACE

Managers are bombarded with advice from consultants, professors, business journalists, and assorted management "gurus" on how to manage their employees. A lot of this advice is well thought out and valuable. Much of it, however, is a gross generalization, ambiguous, inconsistent, or superficial. Some of it is even just downright wrong. Regardless of the quality, there doesn't seem to be any slowdown in the outpouring of this advice. Quite to the contrary. Books on business and management have replaced sex, self-help, and weight loss as topics on many nonfiction best-sellers lists.

I've been teaching and writing about managing people at work for 30 years. As part of my writing efforts, I have read upwards of 25,000 research studies on human behavior. While my practitioner friends are often quick to criticize research and theory-testing, this research has provided us with innumerable insights into human behavior. Unfortunately, to date there has been no short, concise summary of behavioral research that cuts through the jargon to give managers the truth about what works and doesn't work when it comes to managing people at work. Well, this is no longer true. This book has been written to fill that void.

I've organized this book around key, human-behavior-related problem areas that managers face: hiring, motivation, leadership, communication, team building, conflict management, job design, evaluating performance, and coping with change. Within each problem area, I've identified a select set of topics that are relevant to managers and where there is substantial research evidence to draw upon. In addition, I've included suggestions to help readers apply this information to improve their managerial effectiveness. And at the back of the book, I've listed references upon which the chapters are based.

Who was this book written for? Practicing managers and those aspiring to a management position—from CEOs to supervisor wannabes. I wrote it because I believe you shouldn't have to read through detailed textbooks in human resources or organizational behavior to learn the truth about managing people at work. Nor should you have to attend an executive development course at a prestigious university to get the straight facts. What you get from this book, of course, will depend on your current knowledge about organizational behavior. Recent MBAs, for instance, will find this book to be a concise summary of the evidence they spent many months studying. For individuals who haven't kept current with research in organizational behavior or for those with little formal academic training, this book should provide a wealth of new insights into managing people at work.

You'll find each of the 63 topics in this book is given its own short chapter. And each chapter is essentially independent from the others. You can read them in any order you desire. Best of all, you needn't tackle this book in one sitting. It's been designed for multiple "quick reads." Read a few chapters, put it down, then pick it up again at a later date. There's no continuous story line that has to be maintained.

Let me conclude this preface by stating the obvious: A book is a team project. While there is only one name on the cover, a number of people contributed to getting this book in your hands. That team included Tim Moore, Russ Hall, Vanessa Moore, Lawrence Hargett, and Stephanie English.

Stephen P. Robbins
January 2002

PART I

THE TRUTH
ABOUT HIRING

TRUTH 1

FORGET TRAITS;
IT'S BEHAVIOR THAT COUNTS!

You're interviewing applicants to fill a job position in your firm. What are you looking for in these applicants? If you're like many managers, you'll answer with terms such as *hardworking*, *persistent*, *confident*, and *dependable*. After all, how can you go wrong trying to hire people with traits such as these? Well, you can! The problem is that traits aren't necessarily good predictors of future job performance.

Most of us have a strong belief in the power of traits to predict behavior. We know that people behave differently in different situations, but we tend to classify people by their traits, impose judgments about those traits (being self-assured is "good"; being submissive is "bad"), and make evaluations about people based on these trait classifications. Managers often do this when they make hiring decisions or evaluate current employees. After all, if managers truly believed that situations determined behavior, they would hire people almost at random and structure the situation to fit the employee's strengths. But the employee selection process in most organizations places a great deal of emphasis on traits. We see this in the emphasis placed on how applicants perform in interviews and on tests.

During interviews, managers watch and listen to see if applicants have the "qualities" they're looking for in a "good" employee. Similarly, tests are often used to determine the degree to which an applicant has "good employee traits."

There are two problems with using traits in the hiring process. First, organizational settings are strong situations that have a large impact on employee behavior. Second, individuals are highly adaptive and personality traits change in response to organizational situations.

The effects of traits in explaining behavior is likely to be strongest in relatively weak situations and weakest in relatively strong situations. Organizational settings tend to be strong situations because they have rules and other formal regulations that define acceptable behavior and punish deviant behavior, and because they have informal norms that dictate appropriate behaviors. These formal and informal constraints minimize the effects of different personality traits. In contrast, picnics, parties, and similar informal functions are weak situations, and we'd predict that traits would be fairly strong predictors of behavior in these situations.

The best predictor of a person's future behavior is his or her past behavior.

While personality traits are generally stable over time, there is a growing body of evidence that demonstrates that an individual's traits are changed by the organization in which that individual participates. Moreover, people typically belong to multiple organizations (for instance, community, religious, social, athletic, and political, as well as to an employer) that often include very different kinds of members, and they adapt to those different situations. The fact is that people are not prisoners of a rigid and stable personality framework. They can adjust their behavior to reflect the requirements of various situations.

If traits aren't very good for predicting future employee behavior, what should managers use? The answer is: Past behaviors! The best predictor of a person's future behavior is his or her past behavior. So when interviewing candidates, ask questions that focus on previous experiences that are relevant to the current job opening. Here's a couple of examples: "What have you done in previous jobs that demonstrates your creativity?" "On your last job, what was it that you most wanted to accomplish but didn't? Why didn't you?"

TRUTH 2

REALISTIC JOB PREVIEWS:
WHAT YOU SEE IS WHAT YOU GET

Think back to the last time you went for a job interview. Once the interviewer got past asking you questions, how did he or she describe the job and organization? Most managers, when conducting employment interviews, almost exclusively focus on positive aspects. They talk about interesting work assignments, the camaraderie among coworkers, opportunities for advancement, great benefits, and the like. Even though managers typically know the downside of the job and the organization, they carefully avoid those topics. Why turn off a good job applicant by talking about negatives?

Managers who focus only on the positives are making a mistake. They're setting themselves up for the disappointment of a sudden and surprising resignation. All those hours spent reviewing candidate applications and conducting interviews prove wasted when after only a few weeks or a month into the job, the new employee abruptly quits.

Is there anything an astute manager can do to avoid this experience? The answer is Yes: Use realistic job previews.

Realistic job previews provide job applicants with both unfavorable and favorable information before an offer is made.

It's in direct contrast to the typical job previews that most managers give during the interview stage—carefully worded descriptions that sell the positive aspects of the new job and the organization. All these do is set the employee up with false expectations. No job or organization is perfect. And you're more likely to keep your new hires if you're straight with them from the beginning.

When the information that a job applicant receives is excessively inflated, a number of things happen that have potentially negative effects on the organization. First, mismatched applicants who would probably become dissatisfied with the job and soon quit are less likely to select themselves out of the search process. Second, the absence of negative information builds unrealistic expectations. If hired, the new employee is likely to become quickly disappointed. This, in turn, leads to low employee satisfaction and premature resignations.

You're more likely to keep your new hires if you're straight with them from the beginning.

Finally, new hires are prone to becoming disillusioned and less committed to the organization when they come face-to-face with the negatives in the job. No one likes to feel as if they were tricked or misled during the hiring process.

A realistic job preview balances both the positive and negative aspects of the job. For instance, in addition to positive comments, managers could tell candidates that there are limited opportunities to talk with coworkers during work hours, or that erratic fluctuations in workloads create considerable stress on employees during rush periods. Anousheh Ansari, chief operating officer at Telecom Technologies, is a proponent of realistic previews. She says she purposely paints a gloomy picture and tries to scare prospective employees during interviews. For example, she tells them that they'll be expected to put in 10- and 12-hour workdays. "Some people run in the opposite direction, but the ones who stay are committed and willing to do whatever it takes," she says.

The evidence indicates that applicants who have been given a realistic job preview hold lower and more realistic expectations about the job they'll be doing and are better prepared for coping with the job and its frustrating elements. The result is fewer unexpected resignations. While presenting only the positive aspects of a job to a recruit may initially entice him or her to join the organization, it may be a marriage that both you and the new employee will quickly regret.

TRUTH 3

TIPS FOR IMPROVING EMPLOYEE INTERVIEWS

F ew, if any, people are hired without an interview. It's the single most widely used device for screening job candidates. And not only is the interview widely used, it also typically carries a great deal of weight. That is, the results tend to have a disproportionate amount of influence on the decision of who is hired and who isn't.

Effective interviewing skills aren't just for company recruiters or those people who work in an organization's human resources department. Every manager is involved in the hiring process for his or her department. So every manager needs to be capable of conducting effective interviews.

What can you do to be a more effective interviewer? Based on an extensive body of research, here are some helpful hints for improving employee interviews.

First, before meeting an applicant, review his or her application form and résumé. Also review the job description of the position for which the applicant is interviewing. Next, structure the agenda for the interview. Specifically, use a set of standardized questions. That is, you should ask every applicant for a job the same set of questions. Select questions that can't be answered with a simple "yes" or "no." Also avoid leading questions that telegraph the desired response (such as, "Would you say you have good interpersonal skills?"). In most cases, questions relating to marital and family status, age, race, religion, sex, ethnic background, credit rating, and arrest record are prohibited by law in the United States unless you can demonstrate that they are in some way related to job performance. So avoid them. In place of asking, "Are you married?" or "Do you have children?" you might ask, "Are there any reasons why you might not be able to work overtime several times a month?"

Every manager needs to be capable of conducting effective interviews.

When you actually meet the applicant, assume that he or she is nervous and anxious. So put the applicant at ease. Introduce yourself. Be friendly. Begin with a few simple questions or statements that can break the ice. Then preview what topics you plan to discuss, how long the interview will take, and encourage the applicant to ask questions.

The actual interview will be a give-and-take of questions and discussion. The questions you developed during preparation will provide a general road map to guide you. Make sure you cover them all. Follow-up questions should arise from the answers to the standardized questions. These follow-up questions should seek to probe more deeply into what the applicant says. If you feel that the applicant's response is superficial or inadequate, seek elaboration. For instance, to encourage greater response you can say, "Tell me more about that issue." To clarify information, you might say, "You said working overtime was OK, *sometimes*. Can you tell me specifically when you'd be willing to work overtime?" If the applicant doesn't directly answer your question, follow up by repeating the question or paraphrasing it. Importantly, never underestimate the power of silence in an interview. Pause for at least a few seconds after the applicant appears to have finished an answer. Your silence encourages the applicant to continue talking.

Once you're through with the questions and discussions, wrap up the interview. Let the applicant know this fact with a statement such as, "Well, that covers all the questions I have. Is there anything about the job or our organization that I haven't answered for you?" Then let the applicant know what's going to happen next. When can he or she expect to hear from you? Will you write, e-mail, or phone? Are there likely to be more follow-up interviews?

Before you consider the interview complete, write your evaluation while the candidate's comments are fresh in your mind. Now that the applicant is gone, take the time to review your notes and assess the applicant's responses.

TRUTH 4

WANT PLEASANT EMPLOYEES?
IT'S IN THE GENES!

Herb Kelleher, former CEO of Southwest Airlines, recognized what many managers fail to notice: Some people are just inherently more friendly and upbeat than others. Kelleher believes, and rightly so, that it's difficult, if not impossible, to train people to provide friendly and courteous service. So Southwest Airlines focuses its hiring process on selecting out the people who aren't basically happy and outgoing.

A number of jobs—flight attendants, retail clerks, sales people, and customer service are some obvious examples—are performed better by people with positive dispositions. Many managers trying to fill these jobs have assumed that pleasant employees can be created. They spend a lot of their time trying to design motivating jobs, working conditions, or attractive compensation and benefit programs to encourage their employees to be friendly and upbeat. Additionally, they spend millions of dollars on training to shape behavior. Most of these programs fail to achieve their objective. Why? Because whether a person is happy or not is essentially determined by his or her genetic structure. Studies have found that approximately 80 percent of people's differences in happiness is attributable to their genes.

Analysis of satisfaction data for individuals over a 50-year period found that individual results were amazingly stable over time, even when these people changed employers and occupations. This analysis and other evidence suggests that an individual's disposition toward life is established by his or her genetic makeup, that it holds over time, and carries over into his or her disposition toward work.

Approximately 80 percent of people's differences in happiness is attributable to their genes.

The message here is to follow Herb Kelleher's example. If you want pleasant employees, focus your attention on the hiring process. Select out the negative, maladjusted, trouble-making fault finders who derive little satisfaction in anything about their jobs. How? Through personality testing, in-depth interviewing, and careful checking of applicants' previous work records.

TRUTH 5

GOOD CITIZENSHIP COUNTS!

All other things equal, most managers want employees who will do more than their usual job duties. They want employees who will go *beyond* expectations. Employees who exhibit discretionary behavior that is not part of their formal job requirements, but that promotes the organization's operations, are said to be good citizens. And in today's workplace, where flexibility is critical, jobs are fluid, work is often done in teams, and job descriptions frequently fail to include all the essential tasks that need to be done, top performing managers need individuals who display good citizenship behavior.

What *is* good citizenship behavior? Examples include making constructive statements about their work group and the organization, helping others on their team, volunteering for extra job activities, avoiding unnecessary conflicts, showing care for organizational property, respecting the spirit as well as the letter of rules and regulations, and gracefully tolerating the occasional work-related impositions and nuisances. Importantly, studies indicate that those organizational units that have employees who exhibit good citizenship behaviors outperform those that don't.

So what can managers do to stimulate good citizenship among employees? The answer seems to be: Treat people fairly. When people believe out-comes, treatment, and proce-dures are fair, they are more likely to talk positively about the organization, help others, and go beyond the normal expectations in their job. If your employees feel that you, your organization's procedures, and company pay policies are fair, trust is developed. And when

Employees who exhibit good citizenship behaviors outperform those who don't.

they trust you and the organization, they're more willing to voluntarily engage in behaviors that go beyond their formal job requirements.

TRUTH 6

BRAINS MATTER; OR WHEN IN DOUBT, HIRE SMART PEOPLE

Few topics generate more heated discussion and controversy than that of intelligence. People seem to hold widely differing and strong opinions on questions such as: Is IQ a good measure of intelligence? Is intelligence learned or inherited? Are intelligent people more successful than their less-intelligent peers?

We're concerned with the relationship between intelligence and job performance—specifically, do people with higher intelligence outperform their peers with lower intelligence? Not surprisingly, this is a topic in which there is no shortage of opinions. But don't put much weight on opinions. You should look for hard evidence. And there is actually quite a bit of hard evidence to draw upon. Certain facts are beyond significant technical dispute. For instance: (1) IQ score closely matches whatever it is that people mean when they use the word *intelligent* or *smart* in ordinary language; (2) IQ scores are stable, although not perfectly so, over much of a person's life; (3) properly administered IQ tests are not demonstrably biased against social, economic, ethnic, or racial groups; and (4) smarter employees, on average, are more proficient employees. I understand that some of these conclusions may make you uncomfortable or conflict with your personal views, but they are well supported by the research evidence.

All jobs require the use of intelligence or cognitive ability. Why? For reasoning and decision making. High IQs show a strong correlation with performance in jobs that are novel, ambiguous, changing, or

Smarter employees, on average, are more proficient employees.

in multifaceted professional occupations such as accountants, engineers, scientists, architects, and physicians. But IQ is also a good predictor in moderately complex jobs such as crafts, clerical, and police work. IQ is a less valid predictor for unskilled jobs that require only routine decision making or simple problem solving.

Intelligence clearly is not the only factor affecting job performance, but it's often the most important! It is, for example, a better predictor of job performance than a job interview, reference checks, or college transcripts. Unfortunately, the strong genetic component of IQ—probably 70 percent or more of our intelligence is inherited—makes the use of IQ as a selection tool vulnerable to attack. Critics are uncomfortable when average IQs are shown to differ among different races or that IQ has been found to be associated with economic differences. Some critics use these findings to suggest that IQ measures discriminate and, therefore, should be abandoned. This is unfortunate because the evidence overwhelmingly indicates that IQ tests are not biased against particular groups, even though what they measure is largely outside the control of the individual.

• Our conclusion: The race may not always go to the swiftest or the strongest, but that's the way to bet! If you want to hire the best possible workforce, all other things being equal, hire the smartest people you can find.

TRUTH 7

Don't Count Too Much on Reference Checks

Reference checks fall into one of two categories—past work experience and personal. References from past employers tend to be valuable in the hiring process. But unfortunately, they've become increasingly hard to acquire. Personal references, on the other hand, are easy to acquire but they're essentially worthless.

As we noted in Truth 1, the best predictor of future behavior is past behavior. So accurate and reliable information that tells us about a job candidate's past job experience can be a valuable input into the hiring decision. The problem is that employers have become increasingly reluctant to provide anything but the most mundane information to outsiders. In many cases, that information is limited to the former employee's title and dates of employment. The reason for this is simple: U.S. courts hold former employers responsible to release only truthful information. So to protect themselves against lawsuits, employers often provide only minimal details on past employees. Of course this makes it extremely difficult to get the information you most want—that related to the former employee's work performance. In addition, reviews from former employers rarely include unfavorable information. If all the information you get is biased to the positive, that information can't help you very much to differentiate among job candidates. However, to the degree that you're able to find former employers who will speak candidly about a job candidate and provide negative as well as positive information, that information can be valuable in helping you make your selection decision.

There's another concern that also needs to be addressed regarding work-related references. Even if you're able to get valid information on an employee's past performance, you need to be sure to evaluate it in terms of differences that might exist between past jobs and the one you're currently trying to fill. Previous performance levels—both highly positive or negative—don't necessarily transfer from one job to another. A number of external factors may not be common

Personal references are easy to acquire but they're essentially worthless.

between the jobs. For instance, are there comparable resources? Will colleagues and subordinates have similar skills and abilities? Do the organizations evaluate and reward similar criteria? If the jobs and organizations aren't similar, then the ability of past performance to predict future performance is lessened.

Many employers ask job applicants for personal references. Justification for this practice is beyond me. There's no valid reason to believe that these references will help you to identify potentially high-performing employees. The reality is: We all have friends who will say or write positive reviews of us. If every job candidate can provide three "references" who will rave about our ambition, determination, conscientiousness, ability to work with others, and the like, what value do they add to the selection process? The answer is: None.

A final comment: Nothing in this assessment should discourage you from doing a comprehensive background investigation. Confirming a candidate's educational credentials should always be done. So should checking past employers for dates of employment and areas of responsibility. Where employees will be dealing with money or security issues, a check for a possible criminal record is also sensible.

TRUTH 8

WHEN IN DOUBT, HIRE CONSCIENTIOUS PEOPLE!

We know that people don't have common personalities. Some are quiet and passive; others are loud and aggressive. Some are relaxed; others are tense.

An extensive amount of research has identified five basic dimensions that explain the significant variation in human personality. These five factors are

1. Extraversion—Are you an extravert (outgoing, sociable) or an introvert (reserved, timid)?

2. Agreeableness—Are you highly agreeable (cooperative, trusting) or much less so (disagreeable, antagonistic)?

3. Conscientiousness—Are you highly conscientious (responsible, organized) or much less so (unreliable, disorganized)?

4. Emotional stability—Are you stable (calm, self-confident) or unstable (anxious, insecure)?

5. Openness to experience—Are you open to new experiences (creative, curious) or closed (conventional, seek the familiar)?

Numerous studies have been undertaken to see if there is any relationship between these five personality dimensions and job performance. Findings indicate that only conscientiousness is related to job performance. Specifically, conscientiousness predicts job performance across a broad spectrum of jobs—from professionals (engineers, accountants, lawyers) to police, salespeople, and semi-skilled workers. Individuals who score high in conscientiousness are dependable, reliable, careful, thorough, able to plan, organized, hardworking, persistent, and achievement-oriented. And these attributes tend to lead to higher job performance in most occupations.

So if you're looking for a single personality characteristic that is likely to be associated with high job performance, you're well advised to try to hire people who score high on conscientiousness. That, of course, doesn't mean that other characteristics might not be relevant for specific jobs. For instance, evidence indicates that extraversion is a good predictor of performance in managerial and sales positions. This makes sense since these occupations involve a high degree of social interaction.

Conscientiousness predicts job performance across a broad spectrum of jobs—from professionals to police, salespeople, and semi-skilled workers.

Some readers might be surprised that high emotional stability wasn't found to be related to job performance. Intuitively, it would seem that people who are calm and secure would do better on almost all jobs than people who are anxious and insecure. Closer inspection suggests that only people who have fairly high scores on emotional stability retain their jobs. So the range among those people studied, all of whom were employed, tended to be quite small. In other words, people who are low in emotional stability either don't tend to get hired in the first place or, when they do, typically don't last too long in their jobs!

TRUTH 9

HIRE PEOPLE WHO FIT YOUR CULTURE:
MY "GOOD EMPLOYEE" IS YOUR STINKER!

Many a manager has hired a new employee based largely on his or her skills, then lived to regret it. While skill competence is certainly an important ingredient in the making of a "good employee," never underestimate the role that an organization's culture plays in an employee's success or failure. Employee performance typically has a large subjective component. Bosses and colleagues have to make interpretations: Is Dave a team player? Is Tina taking unnecessary risks? Is Laura too competitive? And whether those interpretations are positive or negative depend to a great extent on how well an employee is perceived to fit into the organization. A good fit goes a long way toward ensuring that an employee will be perceived as a high performer.

An organization's culture represents a system of shared meaning. It expresses the core values that are shared by a majority of the organization's members. Microsoft's culture, for example, values aggressiveness and risk taking. In contrast, Johnson & Johnson has a communal culture that emphasizes a strong family feel and values trust and loyalty. The typical "good" employee at Microsoft looks and behaves very differently from the typical "good" employee at J&J.

As a manager, you should assess potential employees in terms of how well you think they will fit into your organization's culture. You want to hire people whose values are essentially consistent with those of the organization, or at least a good portion of those values. If you begin by getting a solid handle on what your organization values and rewards, you're well on your way to determining whether a candidate will be a good match. Ask questions and make observations that will allow you to determine the applicant's propensity to be innovative and take risks, to focus on "the big picture" versus the details, to emphasize means or ends, to be team oriented, to be aggressive and competitive versus easygoing, and whether he or she prefers the status quo to growth. These are the primary elements that identify organizational cultures.

> *Never underestimate the role that an organization's culture plays in an employee's success or failure.*

What can you expect to happen if you make a mistake and hire a few candidates who don't fit with your firm's culture? It's likely you'll wind up with hires who lack motivation and commitment and who are dissatisfied with their jobs and the organization. They'll get lower performance evaluations than employees with similar objective performance but whose

26

values align with the organization. And, not surprisingly, employee "misfits" have considerably higher turnover rates than individuals who perceive a good fit. Most people pick up the cues that they don't fit in and, assuming other job options are available, leave in search of a job where they're more likely to be appreciated.

TRUTH 10

MATCH PERSONALITIES AND JOBS

Want to increase the satisfaction of new employees and decrease the likelihood that they'll resign? There is a substantial amount of evidence that demonstrates this can be achieved by selecting job applicants whose personality matches the job you're trying to fill.

Six personality types have been identified and evidence strongly supports that people are happiest when they are put in jobs that align with their personality. Those six personalities are realistic, investigative, social, conventional, enterprising, and artistic.

A *realistic* person prefers physical activities that require skill, strength, and coordination. Their personality traits: shy, genuine, persistent, stable, conforming, and practical. Examples of jobs that align with their personality include mechanic, drill press operator, assembly-line worker, and farmer.

An *investigative* person prefers activities that involve thinking, organizing, and understanding. Their personality traits: analytical, original, curious, and independent. Examples of job that align with their personality include biologist, economist, software programmer, mathematician, and news reporter.

A *social* person prefers activities that involve helping and developing others. Their personality traits: sociable, friendly, cooperative, and understanding. Examples of jobs that align with their personality include social worker, teacher, counselor, and clinical psychologist.

A *conventional* person prefers rule-regulated, orderly, and unambiguous activities. Their personality traits: conforming, efficient, practical, unimaginative, and inflexible. Examples of jobs that align with their personality include accountant, corporate manager, bank teller, and file clerk.

An *enterprising* person prefers verbal activities in which there are opportunities to influence others and attain power. Their personality traits: self-confident, ambitious, energetic, and domineering. Examples of jobs that align with their personality include lawyer, real estate agent, public-relations specialist, and small-business manager.

An *artistic* person prefers ambiguous and unsystematic activities that allow creative expression. Their personality traits: imaginative, disorderly, idealistic, emotional, and impractical. Examples of jobs that align with their personality include painter, musician, writer, and interior decorator.

People are happiest when they are put in jobs that align with their personality.

The evidence indicates that employee satisfaction is highest and turnover lowest when personality and occupation are in agreement. Social individuals, for instance, should be in social jobs, conventional people in conventional jobs, and so forth. In addition, personalities can be conceptualized in a circle. Points on that circle would be in this order: realistic, investigative, artistic, social, enterprising, conventional, and back to realistic. Findings support that the closer two personalities are in that circle, the more compatible they are. And adjacent categories are most similar. So a realistic person in an investigative job is more congruent—and should be more content—than if he or she were in a social job.

TRUTH 11

MANAGE THE SOCIALIZATION
OF NEW EMPLOYEES

All Marines must go through a multi-week boot camp, where they "prove" their commitment. At the same time, the Marine trainers are indoctrinating new recruits in the "Marine way." In a similar, but less elaborate manner, Starbucks puts all new employees through 24 hours of training to teach them the Starbucks philosophy, the company jargon, and the ins and outs of Starbucks' coffee business.

The Marines and Starbucks use their formal training programs to socialize new members. They're helping employees adapt to their organization's culture. Why? Because no matter how good a job an organization does in recruitment and selection, new employees are not fully indoctrinated in the organization's culture. Socialization turns outsiders into insiders and fine-tunes employee behaviors so they align with what management wants.

When hiring a new employee, you have four decisions to make—each of which will affect the shaping of that new hire's behavior:

First, will socialization be formal or informal? The more a new employee is segregated from the ongoing work setting and differentiated in some way to make explicit his or her newcomer's role, the more formal the socialization is. The Marines and Starbucks' specific orientation and training programs are examples. Informal socialization just puts the new employee directly into his or her job, with little or no special attention.

> *Socialization turns outsiders into insiders and fine-tunes employee behaviors so they align with what management wants.*

Second, will socialization be done individually or collectively? Most employees are socialized individually. But they also can be grouped together and processed through an identical set of experiences as in military boot camp.

Third, will socialization be serial or random? Serial socialization is characterized by the use of role models who train and encourage the newcomer. Apprenticeship and mentoring programs are examples. In random socialization, role models are deliberately withheld. The new employee is left on his or her own to figure things out.

Finally, will socialization seek investiture or diversiture? Investiture assumes that the newcomer's qualities and qualifications are the necessary ingredients for job success, so these qualities and qualifications are confirmed and supported.

Divestiture tries to strip away certain characteristics of the new hire. Fraternity and sorority "pledges" go through divestiture socialization to shape them into the proper role.

Generally speaking, the more that management relies on socialization programs that are formal, collective, serial, and emphasize divestiture, the greater the likelihood that newcomers' differences and perspectives will be stripped away and replaced by standardized and predictable behaviors. Conversely, the use of informal, individual, random, and investiture options will create a workforce of individualists. So managers can use socialization as a tool to create conformists who maintain traditions and customs or, at the other extreme, inventive and creative individuals who consider no organizational practice sacred.

PART II

THE TRUTH
ABOUT
MOTIVATION

TRUTH 12

WHY MANY WORKERS AREN'T MOTIVATED AT WORK TODAY

I often hear experienced managers complain that "people just aren't motivated to work anymore." If this is true, the fault is with managers and organizational practices, not the employees! When employees lack motivation, the problem almost always lies in one of five areas: selection, ambiguous goals, the performance appraisal system, the organization's reward system, or in the manager's inability to shape employee's perception of the appraisal and reward systems.

The best way to understand employee motivation is to think of it as being dependent on three relationships. When all three of these relationships are strong, employees tend to be motivated. If any one or all of these relationships are weak, employee effort is likely to suffer. I'll present these relationships in terms of questions.

First, do employees believe that if they give a maximum effort, it will be recognized in their performance appraisal? For a lot of employees, the answer is unfortunately: No. Why? Their skill level may be deficient, which means that no matter how hard they try, they're not likely to be high performers. Or, if the organization's performance appraisal system is designed to assess nonperformance factors such as loyalty, initiative, or courage, more effort won't necessarily result in a higher appraisal. Still another possibility is that the employee, rightly or wrongly, perceives that he or she is disliked by the boss. As a result, the employee will expect to get a poor appraisal regardless of his or her level of effort. These examples suggest that one possible source of low employee motivation is the employee's belief that no matter how hard he or she works, the likelihood of getting a good performance appraisal is low.

If employees aren't motivated, the fault is with managers and organizational practices, not the employees!

Second, do employees believe that if they get a good performance appraisal, that it will lead to organizational rewards? Many employees see the performance–reward relationship in their job as weak. The reason is that organizations reward a lot of things besides just performance. For example, when pay is allocated to employees on the basis of seniority or "kissing up" to the boss, employees are likely to see the performance–reward relationship as being weak and demotivating.

Last, are the rewards the employees receive the ones that they want? An employee may work hard in hopes of getting a promotion, but gets a pay raise instead. Or an employee wants a more interesting and challenging job, but receives only a few words of praise. Or an employee puts in extra effort, expecting to be relocated to the company's Paris office, but instead is transferred to Phoenix. These examples illustrate the importance of tailoring the rewards to individual employee needs. Sadly, many managers are limited in the rewards they can distribute, so it's difficult for them to individualize rewards. Moreover, some managers incorrectly assume that all employees want the same thing and overlook the motivational effects of differentiating rewards. In either case, employee motivation is suboptimized.

In summary, a lot of employees lack motivation at work because they see a weak relationship between their effort and performance, between performance and organizational rewards, and/or between the rewards they receive and the ones they really want. If you want motivated employees, you need to do what's necessary to strengthen these relationships.

TRUTH 13

HAPPY WORKERS AREN'T NECESSARILY PRODUCTIVE WORKERS!

Doesn't it seem intuitively logical that happy or satisfied workers would be productive workers? Most of us think so. But intuition can often lead you astray and this is one of those cases.

A lot of companies spend serious money in efforts to increase employee job satisfaction. They introduce flexible work hours, provide onsite child care facilities, support generous retirement plans, create architecturally attractive work places, and the like in the hope of increasing employee satisfaction. Then management is disappointed when employee turnover continues to be high and productivity fails to improve. The truth is that while there may be a positive correlation between satisfaction and productivity, it tends to be quite small; in fact, it's more likely that productivity causes satisfaction than the other way around.

A careful review of the evidence finds a correlation of only about +0.14 between satisfaction and productivity. This means that no more than two percent of the variance in output can be accounted for by employee satisfaction. Moreover, the evidence suggests that productive workers are more likely to be happy workers rather than the reverse. That is, productivity leads to satisfaction. If you do a good job, you intrinsically feel positive about it. In addition, if you assume that the organization rewards productivity (which I concede is a big assumption), your higher productivity should increase verbal recognition, your pay level, and probabilities for other rewards. This, in turn, increases your level of satisfaction with the job.

A personal experience might help you see how this works. I've been writing books for more than 25 years. I can honestly say that, in that period, I only had one experience with writer's block. It was back in the early 1980s. I would sit in my office, looking out the window, waiting to "feel like writing." My waiting lasted several weeks. Then one day I had to go in and give a lecture on motivation. When I reviewed the evidence on the relationship between satisfaction and productivity, the answer to my writer's block became immediately evident. The next day, I went into my office and began furiously typing anything that came into my head on the topic at hand. Most of what I wrote was garbage. But there were a few decent sentences. I threw out the garbage and began to work with the decent stuff. Lo and behold, paragraphs of quality material began to flow. And

While there may be a positive correlation between satisfaction and productivity, it tends to be quite small.

the more good stuff I generated, the more enthusiastic I became. Within half a day, my writer's block was gone. The error I had made was assuming that productivity (writing output) would come when I felt good about writing (satisfied). What I needed was to generate some quality output and that would lead to satisfaction.

What are the implications of these findings for managing people? Stop focusing singularly on how you can increase satisfaction. Put your efforts into helping employees become more productive. For instance, consider increasing training expenditures, improving job design, providing better tools, and removing any barriers that might impede an employee being able to do a first-rate job. These actions are then likely to lead to higher employee satisfaction.

TRUTH 14

WORKFORCE GENERATIONS AND VALUES

Do you think Generation X employees—those people born between 1965 and 1980—are different from the Baby Boomers and World War II generations that preceded them? The correct answer is Yes. And understanding these differences are important if you want to maximize the performance of Generation X employees.

Employees in the current U.S. labor force can be segmented by the era in which they entered the work place. They can be placed into one of four groups. Importantly, as we'll show, because people in a common age cohort have had many common experiences, they also tend to share similar values. As we review these four cohorts, keep in mind that our predictions are limited to people born and raised in the United States.

Workers who grew up influenced by the Great Depression, World War II, the Andrews Sisters, and the Berlin blockade entered the workforce throughout the 1950s and early 1960s. They believed in hard work, the status quo, and authority figures. I call them *Veterans*. Once hired, Veterans tended to be loyal to their employer and place great importance on a comfortable life and family security.

Boomers entered the workforce from the mid-1960s through the mid-1980s. This cohort was influenced heavily by the civil rights movement, the Beatles, the Vietnam War, and baby-boom competition. They brought with them a large measure of the "hippie ethic" and distrust of authority. But they also place a great deal of emphasis on achievement and material success. They're pragmatists who believe that ends can justify means. Boomers tend to see the organizations that employ them merely as vehicles for their careers. Values such as a sense of accomplishment and social recognition rank high with them.

Individuals' values differ but tend to reflect the societal values of the period in which they grew up.

Xers' lives have been shaped by globalization, two-career parents, MTV, AIDS, and computers. They value flexibility, life options, and the achievement of job satisfaction. Family and relationships are very important to this cohort. They also enjoy team-oriented work. Money is important as an indicator of career performance, but Xers seem more willing to trade off salary increases, titles, security, and promotions for increased leisure time and expanded lifestyle options. In search of balance in their lives, Xers are less willing to make personal sacrifices for the sake of their employer than previous generations were. Values they rank high include true friendship, happiness, and pleasure.

The most recent entrants to the workforce, the *Nexters*, grew up during prosperous times. So they tend to be optimistic about the economy, believe in themselves, and are confident about their ability to succeed. Nexters are at ease with diversity and are the first generation to take technology for granted. They've lived most of their lives with CD players, VCRs, cellular phones, and the Internet. This generation is very money-oriented and desirous of the things that money can buy. They seek financial success. Like Xers, they enjoy teamwork but they're also highly self-reliant. They tend to emphasize values such as freedom and a comfortable life.

An understanding that individuals' values differ but tend to reflect the societal values of the period in which they grew up can be a valuable aid in understanding and managing employee behavior. Employees in their 60s, for instance, are more likely to accept authority than their coworkers who are 10 or 15 years younger. And workers in their 30s are more likely than their parents to balk at having to work weekends and more prone to leave a job in mid-career to pursue another that provides more leisure time.

TRUTH 15

TELLING EMPLOYEES TO "DO YOUR BEST" ISN'T LIKELY TO ACHIEVE THEIR BEST

A friend of mine, who manages a group of software programmers in Seattle, was recently telling me what a great staff he had and how much faith he had in them. "When I hand out an assignment, I merely tell my people, 'Do your best. No one can ask more of you than that.'" I think my friend was a bit perplexed when I told him that wasn't the best way to motivate his staff. I felt pretty confident in telling him that he would have better success by giving specific and challenging goals to each employee or work team.

There is a mountain of evidence that tells us that people perform best when they have goals. More to the point, we can say that specific goals increase performance; that difficult goals, when accepted, result in higher performance than do easy goals; and that feedback leads to higher performance than does nonfeedback.

Specific hard goals produce a higher level of output than does the generalized goal of "do your best." It's the specificity of the goal itself that acts as an internal stimulus. Goals tell employees what needs to be done and how much effort they'll need to expend to achieve it. For instance, if my Seattle friend's software programmers committed to complete their current project by the last business day of next month, they would now have a specific objective to try to attain. We can say that, all things being equal, the individual or team with a specific goal will outperform his or her counterparts operating with no goals or the generalized goal of "do your best."

If factors such as ability and acceptance of the goals are held constant, we can also state with confidence that the more difficult the goal, the higher the level of performance. More difficult goals encourage people to extend their reach and work harder. Of course, it's logical to assume that easier goals are more likely to be accepted. But once an employee accepts a hard task, he or she is likely to exert a high level of effort to achieve it. The challenge for managers is to have employees see difficult goals as attainable.

> *Specific hard goals produce a higher level of output than does the generalized goal of "do your best."*

There is considerable evidence that tells us that people will do better when they get feedback on how well they're progressing toward their goals because feedback helps to identify discrepancies between what they've accomplished and what they want to do. That is, feedback acts to guide behavior. But all feedback is not equally potent. Self-generated feedback—where an employee is able to monitor his or her

own progress—has been shown to be a more powerful motivator than externally generated feedback from a boss or coworkers.

One final point before we leave this topic: our claims about the power of goals is culture bound. Goals are well adapted to countries such as the United States and Canada because they mesh well with North American cultures. Goals require employees to be reasonably independent and employers to put a high importance on performance. Those requirements are not necessarily true in every country. For instance, don't expect goals to necessarily lead to higher employee performance in countries such as Portugal or Chile.

TRUTH 16

NOT EVERYONE WANTS TO PARTICIPATE IN SETTING THEIR GOALS

Contemporary managers have been well schooled in the importance of using participation—that is, having managers share a significant degree of decision-making power with their employees. The use of participative leadership and decision making have been preached by business schools since the 1960s. For instance, management guru Peter Drucker considered participation in goal-setting to be a necessary part of his Management By Objectives doctrine. Some academics have even proposed that participative management is an ethical imperative.

The last 40 years has seen the decline (and near extinction) of the autocrat, to be replaced by the participative manager. So you might find it surprising that when it comes to setting goals, we discover an interesting finding: It may not matter if employee goals are assigned by the boss or participatively set. The evidence shows little consistent superiority for goals that are set participatively between employees and their bosses over those unilaterally assigned by bosses.

The logic behind participation is well known. As jobs have become more complex, managers rarely know everything their employees do. Thus, participation allows those who know the most to contribute. Participation also increases commitment to decisions. People are less likely to undermine a decision at the time of its implementation if they shared in making that decision. But the evidence doesn't support the idea that participatively set goals are superior to assigned ones. In some cases, participatively set goals achieve superior performance; in other cases, individuals perform best when assigned goals by their boss. The only advantage that participation may provide is that it tends to increase acceptance of a goal. People are more likely to accept even a difficult goal if it is participatively set rather

Participation is no sure means for improving employee performance.

than arbitrarily assigned by their boss. Thus, although participative goals may have no superiority over assigned goals when acceptance is taken as a given, participation does increase the probability that more difficult goals will be agreed to and acted upon.

You may be wondering: Why wouldn't people always do better under participatively set goals? That's a good question. Let me attempt an answer. The explanation may lie in the conditions that are required for participation to be effective. For participation to work, there must be adequate time to participate, the issues in which employees get involved must be relevant to their interests, employees must have the ability (intelligence, technical knowledge, communication skills) to participate, and the organization's culture must support employee involvement. These conditions are not always met in many work places. In addition, while behavioral scientists often ignore this reality, the truth is that many people don't want the responsibilities that come with participation. They prefer to be told what to do and let their boss do the worrying. These conditions and realities may explain why the use of employee participation is no sure means for improving employee performance.

TRUTH 17

Professional Workers Go for the Flow

Can you think of times in your life when you've been so deeply involved in something that nothing else seems to matter? The task consumes you totally and you lose track of time. Most people can. It's most likely to occur when you're doing a favorite activity: running, skiing, dancing, reading a novel, playing a computer game, listening to music, cooking an elegant meal. This totally involved state is called *flow*. Managers should look to flow as a particularly effective way to motivate professional employees.

Research finds that the flow experience itself isn't necessarily a time when people are happy. It's a period of deep concentration. But when a flow task is completed, and the individual looks back on what has happened, he or she is flooded with feelings of gratitude for the experience. It's then that the person realizes the satisfaction received from the experience and how it made them happier.

Are there conditions that are likely to produce flow? Yes. When people describe flow experiences, they talk about common characteristics in the tasks they were doing. The tasks were challenging and required using a high level of skills. The tasks were goal-directed and provided them with feedback on how well they were performing. The tasks also demanded total concentration and creativity. And the tasks were so consuming that people had no attention left over to think about anything irrelevant or to worry about problems.

Here's something that might surprise you: The flow experience is rarely reported by people when they're doing leisure activities such as watching television or relaxing. Flow is *most likely* to be experienced *at work*, not at home!

If you ask people whether they'd like to work less, the answer is almost always yes. People associate leisure with happiness. They think if they had more free time, they'd be happier. Studies of thousands of individuals suggest that people are generally wrong in this belief. When people spend time at home, for instance, they often lack a clear purpose,

Flow is most likely to be experienced at work, not at home!

don't know how well they're doing, get distracted, and feel that their skills are underutilized. They frequently describe themselves as bored. But work has many of the properties that stimulate flow. It usually has clear goals. It provides people with feedback on how well they're doing—either from the work process itself or through a boss's evaluation. People's skills are typically matched to their jobs, which provides challenge. And jobs usually encourage concentration and prevent distractions.

The end result is that work, rather than leisure, more clearly mirrors the flow that people might get from games, sport, music, or art.

What are the managerial implications from flow research? Work, itself, can be a powerful motivator. It can provide a feeling of happiness that most leisure activities can't. So, where possible, design jobs with challenging, creative, and consuming tasks that allow employees to utilize their skills, and ensure that these tasks have clear goals and provide employees with feedback.

TRUTH 18

Watch Out for Cyberloafing!

Are employees at their computers always *working* at their computers? The answer is increasingly: No! The average U.S. employee with Internet access is spending 90 minutes a day visiting Web sites unrelated to his or her job. And Canadian employees are wasting about 800 million work hours a year surfing the Web for personal reasons. These employees are e-mailing friends, shopping online, stock trading, searching for jobs, and playing games. Some of the most visited U.S. sites people access from work include the Weather Channel, Amazon.com, and eBay.

In one recent month, Pogo.com reported that over a million people visited its game site from work. And the average workplace player spent more than 2 hours and 30 minutes per visit glued to a Pogo.com game! As a 24-year-old tech-support worker in Dallas casually put it, "It would never occur to me to play Pogo when I'm not at work."

If the work itself isn't interesting or creates excessive stress, employees are likely to be motivated to do something else. If they have easy access to the Internet, that "something else" is increasingly using the Net as a diversion. Unfortunately, this diversion or "cyberloafing" is costing U.S. employers $54 billion a year in lost productivity.

The solution to cyberloafing includes making jobs interesting to employees, providing formal breaks to overcome monotony, and establishing clear guidelines so employees know what online behaviors are expected. Many employers are also installing sophisticated surveillance software that can monitor the behavior of employees who do their work on computers. Xerox, as a case in point, routinely monitors the Web activities of every one of its employees around the world. In October 1999, the company fired 40 of its employees because they were caught in the act of surfing to forbidden Web sites. The company's monitoring software recorded the unauthorized visits to shopping and pornography sites, and every minute they had spent at those sites.

> *The average U.S. employee with Internet access is spending 90 minutes a day visiting Web sites unrelated to his or her job.*

Xerox isn't unique. A recent survey by the American Management Association found that 54 percent of employers monitor their employees' Internet usage and 38 percent read their employees' e-mail. Is this behavior wrong or unethical? Not as long as employees have clear guidelines regarding expectations and know ahead of time that this monitoring is being done. As a manager, you need to be assured that your employees are working and not goofing off; that employees are not distributing organization secrets; and that your organization is protected against employees who might create a hostile environment for women or members of minority groups by sending inappropriate messages over the organization's intranet or Internet links.

TRUTH 19

WHEN GIVING FEEDBACK: CRITICIZE BEHAVIORS, NOT PEOPLE

It seems pretty simple but it's amazing how many managers ignore this advice when giving feedback to employees: Criticize employee behaviors, not the people themselves. Successful feedback focuses on specific behavior and is impersonal.

Feedback should be specific rather than general. Managers should avoid making statements like "You have a bad attitude" or "I'm really impressed with the good job you did." These types of statements are vague and, while they provide information, they don't tell the employee enough to correct the "bad attitude" or on *what basis* it was concluded that a "good job" had been done. For clarity, here are some examples of what good feedback is like: "Bob, I'm concerned with your attitude toward your work. You were a half-hour late to yesterday's staff meeting, and then you told me you hadn't read the preliminary report we were discussing. Today you tell me you're taking off three hours early for a dental appointment"; or "Jan, I was really pleased with the job you did on the Phillips account. They increased their purchases from us by 22 percent last month and I got a call a few days ago from Dan Phillips complimenting me on how quickly you responded to those specification changes for the MJ-7 microchip." Both of these statements focus on specific behaviors. They tell the recipient *why* you are being critical or complimentary.

In addition, feedback—especially the negative kind—should be descriptive rather than judgmental or evaluative. No matter how upset a manager might be, for instance, he or she should keep the feedback job-related and never criticize someone personally because of an inappropriate action. Telling people they're "stupid," "incompetent," or the like is almost always counterproductive. It provokes such an emotional reaction that the performance deviation itself is apt to be overlooked. When a manager is criticizing an employee, that manager is censuring a job-related behavior, not the person. You may be tempted to tell someone he or she is "rude and insensitive" (which may be true); however, that's hardly impersonal. Better to say something like "You interrupted me three times, with questions that were not urgent, when you knew I was talking long distance to a customer in Ireland."

> *Successful feedback focuses on specific behavior and is impersonal.*

One final point on feedback: If negative, make sure the behavior is controllable by the recipient. There's little constructive value in reminding a person of some shortcoming over which he or she has no control. Negative feedback, therefore, should be directed toward behavior the recipient can do something about. So, for example, to criticize an employee who is late because he forgot to set his wake-up alarm is valid. To criticize him for being late when the subway he takes to work every day had a power failure, trapping him underground for half an hour, is pointless. There is nothing he could do to correct what happened.

TRUTH 20

YOU GET WHAT YOU REWARD

A management consultant specializing in police research noticed that, in one community, officers would come on duty for their shift, proceed to get into their police cars, drive to the highway that cut through the town, and speed back and forth along this highway for their entire shift. Clearly this fast cruising had little to do with good police work. But this behavior made considerably more sense once the consultant learned that the community's city council used mileage on police vehicles as a measure of police effectiveness. The city council unintentionally was rewarding "putting lots of miles on police cars," so that's what officers emphasized.

Managers routinely reward employee behaviors they're trying to discourage and fail to reward the behaviors they actually want. A few examples illustrate this sad fact: Management says it wants to build teamwork, actually rewards individual accomplishments, then wonders why employees compete against each other and are constantly looking out for Number One. Management talks up the importance of quality, then ignores employees who turn out shoddy work and punishes those who fail to meet their production goals because they're focusing on quality. Senior executives speak out loudly about the importance of their managers acting ethically, then give a big promotion to a manager whose ethical conduct is clearly suspect.

Managers who claim that their employees seem to be lacking motivation should review their reward systems to consider the possibility that they're paying off for behavior other than what they're seeking. This review should begin by assessing what types of behaviors are currently being rewarded. What this assessment too often finds is that organizations are not rewarding what they assume they are. Obviously, if this is the case, then the reward system needs to be changed to get the desired behaviors. If you want quality, reward quality. If you want ethical behavior, then reward employees who act ethically.

Modifying reward systems doesn't have to be a complex undertaking. Small adjustments can make big differences. And the little techniques you use at home can often be applied at the workplace. For instance, if you buy a single candy bar for your two kids, can you expect them to fight over who gets which half? Probably. Have you ever just given the candy bar to one of them, told him to cut it in half, and then let his brother or sister have first choice on which half he or she wants? This simple process of rewarding joint responsibility typically results in a precise and fair slicing up of the candy bar and a marked decline in fighting. This same logic was recently used by a department head who had to allocate offices in the company's new building. Two of his employees, who had never gotten along, were wasting a lot of time arguing which one of the 10 offices allocated to the department each would take. It seemed that whichever one Dave wanted, that would also be the one that Chuck preferred. After weeks of haggling, the department head told Dave to make two choices and that he was going to let Chuck make the first selection and Dave would get the other. The end result was that Dave sought two offices that were both acceptable to him, Chuck got "the pick of the litter," and both were happy.

One last comment. The importance of rewarding the right behaviors never was clearer to me than when I saw a rich relative continually tell her son, "Don't worry about saving money. You'll have plenty when I'm gone." That relative lived a very long life and she could never understand why her son looked forward to her demise. Clearly she would have gotten a very different behavior from her son had she made his inheritance conditioned on her longevity. He would have been far more supportive of her living a long life had she said in her latter years, "I'm going to give you $50,000 the first of every year for as long as I live. But when I go, all my remaining money will go to charity." Had she taken this approach, her son would have a vested interest in prolonging her life, not shortening it!

Managers routinely reward employee behaviors they're trying to discourage and fail to reward the behaviors they actually want.

TRUTH 21

IT'S ALL RELATIVE!

A major league baseball player tells his team that he won't be reporting to spring training. Although he's under contract, and scheduled to make $7.5 million dollars this season, he says he's not motivated to play this year. He wants his team to either renegotiate his contract or trade him so he can get more money. Neither this player nor his agent ever suggests that $7.5 million is inadequate to live on. The argument is almost always couched in terms of relative rewards: "Other players who aren't as good as I am [haven't played as long; haven't won as many games; don't have as impressive statistics] are earning more."

There is an impressive body of evidence that tells us that employees don't only look at absolute rewards. They look at relative rewards. They compare what inputs they bring to a job (in terms of experience, effort, education, and competence) with the outcomes they receive (salary levels, pay raises, recognition, and the like). Then they look around for other references to compare themselves against. Those other references may be friends, relatives, neighbors, coworkers, colleagues in other organizations, or past jobs they have had.

Finally, they compare their input/outcome ratio with the others and assess how equitably they think they're being treated. For our baseball player, he looks at his pay and his statistics; compares them with similar professional players at his position; and cries "foul" because he thinks he's under-rewarded.

When people makes these comparisons, they come to one of three conclusions: They're either being *fairly treated, under-rewarded*, or *over-rewarded*. Fair treatment has a positive effect on motivation. Employees are likely to be motivated when they feel they are being equitably rewarded for their contribution.

People seem to have a great deal more tolerance of overpayment inequities than underpayment, or they're better able to rationalize them.

However, when people perceive themselves as being under-rewarded, they tend to get angry. To lessen this anger and restore equity, they are likely to engage in behaviors or perception adjustments. For instance, they might take more paid sick leave, come in late to work or leave early, take longer breaks, put out less effort, ask for a raise, or even steal from the company in an attempt to "get what's mine." They might also reassess either their own or others' inputs and outcomes, or change the person or persons with which they're comparing themselves. At the extreme, under-rewarded employees can become angry enough to quit.

The degree of active behavior that under-rewarded employees will take is largely dependent on how equity-sensitive they are. Some employees are very good at ignoring inequities or adjusting their perceptions to make them less bothersome. But many professional and technical employees are quite equity-sensitive. They're likely to move quickly to correct any perceived inequity.

When people perceive themselves as over-rewarded, they react with guilt. And to relieve that guilt, they might work harder, get more education, help out others, or work through a paid vacation. Not surprisingly, the guilt rarely leads to requests for reductions in pay. In fact, people seem to have a great deal more tolerance of overpayment inequities than underpayment, or they're better able to rationalize them.

TRUTH 22

RECOGNITION MOTIVATES
(AND IT COSTS VERY LITTLE!)

A few years back, 1,500 employees in a variety of work settings were surveyed to find out what they considered to be the most powerful workplace motivator. Their response? Recognition, recognition, and more recognition! Another study found that employees rated personal thanks from a manager for a job well done as the most motivating of a variety of incentives offered. But, unfortunately, 58 percent of the workers in this study said their managers didn't typically give such thanks.

In today's highly competitive global economy, most organizations are under severe cost pressures. That makes recognition programs particularly attractive. Why? In contrast to most other motivators, recognizing an employee's superior performance often costs little or no money. Maybe that's why a recent survey of 3,000 employers found that two-thirds use or plan to use special recognition awards. Recognition has been found to be especially relevant in the motivation of low-wage workers. It costs little and helps to build employee self-esteem. For instance, Fine Host Corp., a food service firm in Connecticut, gives out quality awards and posts workers' names in company buildings to recognize good work. All Metro Health Care in Lynbrook, New York, sponsors an award for home health caregiver of the year and also gives employees gifts, such as watches and blenders, for scoring high in quarterly training exercises.

We have a wealth of evidence that tells us that rewarding a behavior with recognition immediately following that behavior is likely to encourage its repetition. How can managers use this to help motivate employees? They can personally congratulate an employee in private for a good job. They can send a handwritten note or an e-mail message acknowledging something positive that the employee has done. For employees with a strong need for social acceptance, managers can publicly recognize accomplishments.

The most powerful workplace motivator? Recognition, recognition, and more recognition!

And to enhance group cohesiveness and motivation, managers can celebrate team successes. They can use meetings to recognize the contributions and achievements of successful work teams.

And keep in mind, little things can mean a lot. Lee Memorial Health System, in Cape Coral, Florida, found this out when it gave customized key chains to each of its 5,000 employees as a "thank you" when *Modern Healthcare* magazine named Lee as one of the top 100 integrated health care networks in the United States. The key chains, designed especially for Lee Memorial, had the words "Valued Employee Since" displayed on the top of a brass emblem and the employee's year of hire added below. They cost Lee only $4.50 per employee, but they proved to be a powerful motivator. Lee's CEO said, "In all my years in health care administration, I've never witnessed as much excitement as was created by giving the key chains to our staff. I received many thank you notes and e-mails expressing appreciation that we would take the time to recognize each employee individually."

TRUTH 23

WAYS TO MOTIVATE LOW-SKILL, LOW-PAY EMPLOYEES

One of the most challenging motivation problems for managers in industries such as retailing and fast food is: How do you motivate individuals who are making very low wages and who have little opportunity to significantly increase their pay in either their current jobs or through promotion? These jobs are typically filled with people who have limited education and skills, and pay levels are little above minimum wage. And given the reality that the public isn't likely to warm up to paying $10 for a Big Mac, employers can't afford to pay these employees much above $6 or $7 an hour.

Traditional approaches for motivating these people have focused on providing more flexible work schedules and filling these jobs with teenagers and retirees whose financial needs are less. This has met with less than enthusiastic results. For instance, turnover rates of 200 percent or more are not uncommon for businesses such as McDonald's. Taco Bell has tried to make some of its service jobs more interesting and challenging but with limited results. It has experimented with incentive pay and stock options for cashiers and cooks. These employees also have been given broader responsibility for inventory, scheduling, and hiring. But over a four-year period, this experiment has only reduced annual turnover from 223 percent to 160 percent.

What choices are left? Unless pay and benefits are significantly increased, high turnover probably has to be expected in these jobs. This can be somewhat offset by widening the recruiting net, making these jobs more appealing, providing employees with considerable flexibility around work hours, and raising pay levels. You might also try some nontraditional approaches as well. For example, Judy Wicks has found that celebrating employees' outside interests has dramatically cut turnover among waiters at her White Dog Café in Philadelphia. To help create a close and family-like work climate, Wicks sets aside one night a year for employees to share their personal lives with coworkers—exhibiting their art, reading their poetry, explaining their volunteer work, and introducing their new babies.

Annual turnover rates of 200 percent or more are not uncommon for businesses such as McDonald's.

TRUTH 24

There's More to High Employee Performance Than Just Motivation

Robin and Chris both graduated from college a couple of years ago with degrees in elementary education. They each took jobs as first grade teachers but in different school districts. Robin immediately confronted a number of obstacles on the job: a large class (38 students), a small and dingy classroom, and inadequate supplies. Chris's situation couldn't have been more different. He had only 15 students in his class, plus a teaching aide for 15 hours each week, a modern and well-lighted room, a well-stocked supply cabinet, an iMac computer for each student, and a highly supportive principal. Not surprisingly, at the end of the first school year, Chris had been considerably more effective as a teacher than had Robin.

The preceding episode illustrates an obvious but often overlooked fact: Success on a job is facilitated or hindered by the existence or absence of support resources. No matter how motivated an employee is, his or her performance is going to suffer if there isn't a supportive work environment.

A popular way of thinking about employee performance is as a function of the interaction of ability and motivation; that is, performance $= f(A \times M)$. If either ability or motivation is inadequate, performance will be negatively affected. This helps to explain, for instance, the hardworking athlete with modest abilities who consistently outperforms his or her more gifted, but lazy, rivals. But an important piece of the performance puzzle is still missing. We need to add opportunity to our equation. Performance $= f(A \times M \times O)$. Even though an individual may be willing and able, there may be obstacles that constrain performance.

No matter how motivated an employee is, his or her performance is going to suffer if there isn't a supportive work environment.

When you attempt to assess why an employee may not be performing to the level that you believe he or she is capable of, take a look at the work environment to see if it's supportive. Does the employee have adequate tools, equipment, materials, and supplies? Does the employee have favorable working conditions, helpful coworkers, supportive work rules and procedures, sufficient information to make job-related decisions, adequate time to do a good job, and the like? If not, performance will suffer.

PART III

THE TRUTH
ABOUT LEADERSHIP

TRUTH 25

THE ESSENCE OF LEADERSHIP IS TRUST

Morale has plummeted at Chrysler's suburban Detroit headquarters. And it's largely due to recent comments by DaimlerChrysler Chairman Jurgen Schrempp. When Daimler-Benz and Chrysler merged in 1998, Schrempp called it "a merger of equals." But in fall of 2000, he admitted he lied. Schrempp now says he never really intended for the combined companies to be equals. If he had been honest, he says, there would have been no deal and he couldn't have made Chrysler into just another Daimler operating unit. With these words, Schrempp has decimated any trust that he may have had with his Chrysler employees.

When we trust someone, we assume they'll act honestly and truthfully, and be reliable and predictable. We also assume they won't take advantage of our trust. Trust is the essence of leadership because it's impossible to lead people who don't trust you.

One author summarized the link between trust and leadership this way: "Part of the leader's task has been, and continues to be, working with people to find and solve problems, but whether leaders gain access to the knowledge and creative thinking they need to solve problems depends on how much people trust them. Trust and trust-worthiness modulate the leader's access to knowledge and cooperation."

When employees trust a leader, they're willing to be vulnerable to the leader's actions—confident that their rights and interests will not be abused. People are unlikely to look up to or follow someone whom they perceive as dishonest or who is likely to take advantage of them. Honesty, for instance, consistently ranks at the top of most people's list of characteristics they admire in their leaders. It's an absolutely essential component of leadership.

Now, maybe more than any time in the past, managerial and leadership effectiveness depends on the ability to gain the trust of followers. Why? Because in times of change and instability—which characterizes most workplaces today—people turn to personal relationships for guidance, and the quality of these relationships is largely determined by the level of trust. In addition, contemporary management practices such as empowerment and the use of work teams require trust to be effective.

So how do you, as a manager, get employees to trust you? It's no simple task but there are actions that research indicates help to build trusting relationships:

Be open. Mistrust comes as much from what people don't know as from what they do know. Keep people informed, make the criteria on how decisions are made overtly clear, explain the rationale for your decisions, be candid about problems, and fully disclose relevant information.

Be fair. Before making decisions or taking actions, consider how others will perceive them in terms of

The Truth About Managing People . . . and Nothing but the Truth

objectivity and fairness. Give credit where it's due, be objective and impartial in performance appraisals, and pay attention to equity perceptions in reward distributions.

Speak your feelings. Managers who convey only hard facts come across as cold and distant. If you share your feelings, others will see you as real and human.

> It's impossible to lead people who don't trust you.

Tell the truth. Truth is an inherent part of integrity. Once you have lied and been found out, your ability to gain and hold trust is largely diminished. People are generally more tolerant of learning something they "don't want to hear" than finding out that their manager lied to them.

Show consistency. People want predictability. Mistrust comes from not knowing what to expect. Let your central values and beliefs guide your actions. This increases consistency and builds trust.

Fulfill your promises. Trust requires that people believe that you are dependable. So you need to ensure that you keep your word and commitments.

Maintain confidences. People trust those who are discreet and upon whom they can rely. They need to feel assured that you will not discuss their confidences with others or betray that confidence. If people perceive you as someone who leaks personal confidences or someone who can't be depended on, you won't be perceived as trustworthy.

TRUTH 26

EXPERIENCE COUNTS! WRONG!

Most of us accept the commonsense notion that experience is a valuable, even necessary, component for effective leadership. Voters, for instance, tend to believe that the jobs of U.S. senator or state governor prepare individuals to be effective U.S. presidents. Similarly, organizations buy into this notion when they carefully screen outside candidates for senior management positions on the basis of their experience. For that matter, have you ever filled out an employment application that *didn't* ask about previous experience or job history? In many instances, experience is the single most important factor in hiring and promotion decisions. Well, here's the surprising news: the evidence doesn't support that experience per se contributes to leadership effectiveness.

"Some inexperienced leaders have been outstandingly successful, while many experienced leaders have been outstanding failures. Among the most highly regarded former presidents are Abraham Lincoln and Harry Truman, who had very little previous leadership, while highly experienced Herbert Hoover and Franklin Pierce were among the least successful."

Studies of military officers, research and development teams, shop supervisors, post office administrators, and school principals tell us that experienced managers tend to be no more effective than the managers with little experience.

How could it be that experience wouldn't make leaders more effective? Intuitively, it would seem that experience would provide learning opportunities that would translate into improved on-the-job leadership skills. The problems seem to be twofold. First, quality of experience and time in the job are not necessarily the same thing. Second, there is variability between situations that influence the transferability of experience.

One flaw in the "experience counts" logic is the assumption that length of time on a job is actually a measure of experience. This says nothing about the quality of experience. The fact that one person has 20 years' experience while another has two years' doesn't necessarily mean that the former has had 10 times as many meaningful experiences. Too often, 20 years of experience is nothing other than one year of experience repeated 20 times! In even the most complex jobs, real learning typically ends after about two years. By then, almost all new and unique situations have been experienced. So one problem with trying to link experience with leadership effectiveness is not paying attention to the quality and diversity of the experience.

Too often, 20 years of experience is nothing other than one year of experience repeated 20 times!

Moreover, the situation in which experience is obtained is rarely comparable to new situations. It's critical to take into consideration the relevance of past experience to a new situation. Jobs differ, support resources differ, organizational cultures differ, follower characteristics differ, and so on. A primary reason that leadership experience isn't strongly related to leadership performance is undoubtedly due to variability of situations.

So what can we conclude? When selecting people for leadership positions, be careful not to place too much emphasis on their experience. Experience, per se, is not a very good predictor of effectiveness. Just because a candidate has 10 years of previous leadership experience is no assurance that his or her experience will transfer to a new situation. What *is* relevant is the quality of previous experience and the relevance of that experience to the new situation that the leader will face.

TRUTH 27

MOST PEOPLE THINK THEY KNOW WHAT GOOD LEADERS LOOK LIKE

Despite all the studies that have been done trying to find out what makes an effective leader, the fact remains that there is still a great deal that we don't understand. For instance, there seem to be very few, if any, traits that continually differentiate leaders from nonleaders. And there is a lot of conflicting evidence that makes it hard to generalize from. But here's an interesting twist: While leadership researchers may have difficulty agreeing on what makes a leader, the average person on the street doesn't seem to have that problem. Lay people (including many managers and senior executives!) have little difficulty describing what they *think* leaders look like. People regularly identify effective leaders as having common traits such as intelligence, outgoing personalities, strong verbal skills, aggressiveness, and industriousness. In addition, effective leaders are generally thought to be consistent or unwavering in their decisions. Debates among U.S. presidential candidates and assessments of the performance of U.S. presidents provide illustrative examples.

Every four years, Americans vote to elect a president. Since 1960, these elections have been preceded by widely televised debates. Presidential candidates spend 90 minutes or so discussing issues, responding to questions, and trying to "look presidential." Looking like a leader in these beauty contests is viewed by the candidates and their staffs as critical to a campaign's success. The eventual losses by Richard Nixon (1960), Gerald Ford (1976), Michael Dukakis (1988), and Al Gore (2000) have often been attributed to their inability to project the leadership traits that the television audience was looking for in their next president. Voters seem to look

Even if you can't be a leader, you can at least LOOK like one!

for certain "leader" traits in their presidents—such as determinedness, decisiveness, and truthworthiness—and they use the debates as an important indicator of whether candidates have those traits. Similarly, one of the explanations of why Ronald Reagan (during his first term as president) was perceived as a leader was that he was fully committed, steadfast, and consistent in the decisions he made and the goals he set. George Herbert Bush, in contrast, undermined the public's perception of his leadership by increasing income taxes after stating categorically during his campaign: "Read my lips. No new taxes."

The message here is somewhat Machiavellian: Even if you can't *be* a leader, you can at least *look* like one! You can attempt to shape the perception that you're smart, personable, decisive, verbally adept, aggressive, hard-working, and consistent in your statements and actions. Will this guarantee leadership success? That we can't say. But if you can successfully project these traits, you'll increase the likelihood that your bosses, colleagues, and employees will *view you* as someone who is an effective leader.

TRUTH 28

EFFECTIVE LEADERS KNOW
HOW TO FRAME ISSUES

M artin Luther King, Jr.'s "I Have a Dream" speech largely shaped the civil rights movement. His words created an imagery of what a country would be like where racial prejudice no longer existed; that is, King *framed* the civil rights movement in a way so others would see it the way he saw it.

Framing is a way to use language to manage meaning. It's a way for leaders to influence how events are seen and understood. It involves the selection and highlighting of one or more aspects of a subject while excluding others.

Framing is analogous to what a photographer does. The visual world that exists is essentially ambiguous. When a photographer aims her camera and focuses on a specific shot, she frames her photo. Others then see what she wanted them to see. They see her point of view. That is precisely what leaders do when they frame an issue. They choose which aspects or portion of the subject they want others to focus on and which portions they want to be excluded.

Political leaders live or die on their ability to frame problems and their opponent's image. In an age of language wars, political victory often goes to those who win the battle over terminology. George W. Bush, for instance, talks about "opportunity scholarships" rather than the unpopular concept of school vouchers, and sought repeal of the "death tax" rather than the "estate tax." And when Bush proposed a $1.6 trillion tax cut, he called it a "refund" for overcharged Americans. That sounds a lot fairer than a "tax cut that overwhelmingly benefits the rich."

In the complex and chaotic environment in which most leaders work, there is typically considerable maneuverability with respect to "the facts." What is real is often what the leader says is real. What's important is what he or she chooses to say is important. Leaders can use language to influence followers' perceptions of the world, the meaning of events, beliefs about causes and consequences, and visions of the future. So a leader's effectiveness is strongly influenced by his or her ability to frame issues.

Framing influences leadership effectiveness in numerous ways. It largely shapes the decision process in that frames determine the problems that need attention, the causes attributed to the problems, and the eventual choices for solving the problems. Framing also increases a leaders' success in implementing goals and getting people's agreement, because once the right frames are in place, the right behavior follows. In addition, framing is critical to effective leadership in a global context because leaders must frame problems in common ways to prevent cultural misunderstandings. Finally, of course, framing is a vital element in visionary leadership. Shared visions are achieved through common framing.

There are five language forms that can help you frame issues—metaphors, jargon, contrast, spin, and stories.

Metaphors help us understand one thing in terms of another. They work well when the standard of comparison is well understood and links logically to something else. When a manufacturing executive describes his goal of having "our production process running like a fine Swiss watch," he is using a metaphor to help his employees envision his ideal.

Organizational leaders are fond of using *jargon*. This is language that is peculiar to a particular profession, organization, or specific program. It conveys accurate meaning only to those who know the vernacular. Bell Atlantic (now part of Verizon) used exercises such as "breaking the squares" and "finding the blue chips" in employee training sessions and they became symbols within the company for finding new ways of thinking and identifying priority assignments, respectively. When a manager says that "this project is a blue chip assignment," people know that it's important and should get priority.

> *Political leaders live or die on their ability to frame problems and their opponent's image.*

When leaders use the *contrast* technique, they illuminate a subject in terms of its opposite. Why? Because sometimes it's easier to say what a subject is *not* more easily than what it is. When an executive at a small software company was frustrated by his employees' lack of concern with keeping costs down, he constantly chided them with the phrase, "we're not Microsoft." The message he wanted to convey was that his company didn't have the financial resources of the software giant and they needed to reduce costs.

Presidential politics has created a new term—*spin*. Those who practice the art are called *spin doctors*. The objective of this technique is to cast your subject in a positive or negative light. Leaders who are good at "spinning" get others to interpret their interests in positive terms and opposing interests in negative terms. They emphasize their strengths and their opponent's weaknesses. When executives at British Airways and American Airlines announced plans to cooperate on U.S.–U.K. routes, they gave it a positive spin by promoting the advantages to consumers. Richard Branson, head of Virgin Airlines and a direct competitor on these routes, responded with a negative spin—emphasizing the monopolistic implications and the downside effects on consumers.

Finally, leaders use *stories* to frame issues with examples that are larger than metaphors or jargon. When leaders at 3M continually retell the story of how Post-it Notes were discovered, they remind people of the importance the company places on creativity and serendipity in the innovation process.

TRUTH 29

You Get What You Expect

Let me tell you about 105 Israeli soldiers who were participating in a combat command course. The four instructors in this course were told that one-third of the specific incoming trainees had high potential, one-third had normal potential, and the potential of the rest was unknown. In reality, the trainees were randomly placed into these categories by researchers conducting the study. In spite of the fact that the three groups should have performed about equally, since they were randomly placed, those trainees who instructors were told had high potential scored significantly higher on objective achievement tests, exhibited more positive attitudes, and held their leaders in higher regard than did the others.

What happened here illustrates the power of expectations. The instructors of the supposedly high-potential trainees got better results from them because the instructors expected it!

Think of expectations as sort of a self-fulfilling prophesy. Expectations of how someone is likely to act cause that person to fulfill the expectation. In business, this tells us that managers get the performance they expect. Treat someone as a loser and they won't disappoint you. Treat them as capable individuals who can perform at the highest level and they'll do their best to prove you right. Leaders who expect more get more!

Why do high employee expectations lead to higher performance? Because a leader's expectations influence the leader's behavior toward employees. Leaders allocate resources to employees in proportion to their expectations. They invest their best leadership in those they expect to perform best. Employees who a leader expects to do well receive more emotional support through nonverbal cues (like smiling and eye contact), more frequent and valuable feedback, more challenging goals, better training, and more desirable assignments. And leaders exhibit greater trust in these employees. These behaviors, in turn, lead to employees who are better trained, with better skills

Treat someone as a loser and they won't disappoint you.

and job knowledge. In addition, the leader's support helps build employee confidence, which increases the employee's belief that he or she can succeed on the job.

The message here for leaders is that you should expect high performance from your employees. Tell them verbally and show them by your behavior that you believe in them. Let them know that you think they have untapped potential and that they can achieve more than they have. But don't expect *too much*. Sky-high expectations can be intimidating and demoralizing—leading to frustration, failure, and low expectations in the future. If you help employees achieve "small wins," they'll build their confidence and gradually raise their expectations over time.

TRUTH 30

GREAT FOLLOWERS
MAKE GREAT LEADERS

An executive was once asked: "What makes a great leader?" His answer was: "Great followers!" Although he was being a bit flippant, there was some truth in his answer. Leaders get things done through others. And no matter what a leader does, if followers don't respond, then the leader fails. So successful leaders *do* have successful followers.

Is there anything you should look for in employees that might increase the likelihood that they'll make good followers? Yes!

They manage themselves well. Effective followers are able to think for themselves. They can work independently and without close supervision.

They are committed to a purpose outside themselves. Effective followers are committed to something—a cause, a product, a work team, an organization, an idea—in addition to the care of their own lives. Most people like working with colleagues who are emotionally, as well as physically, committed to their work.

They build their competence and focus their efforts for maximum impact. Effective followers master skills that will be useful to their organizations, and they hold higher performance standards than their job or work group requires.

No matter what a leader does, if followers don't respond, then the leader fails.

They are courageous, honest, and credible. Effective followers establish themselves as independent, critical thinkers whose knowledge and judgment can be trusted. They hold high ethical standards, give credit where credit is due, and aren't afraid to admit their mistakes.

TRUTH 31

CHARISMA CAN BE LEARNED

There is an increasing amount of evidence that supports the value of charisma in leadership. Many of our most visible leaders, both past and present, have stood out for their charismatic qualities. These would include individuals such as John F. Kennedy, Mahatma Gandhi, Martin Luther King, Jr., Steve Jobs, Mary Kay Ash, Ted Turner, Richard Branson, Margaret Thatcher, and Bill Clinton.

What differentiates these charismatic leaders from their noncharismatic counterparts? Common characteristics of charismatic leaders include self-confidence, a strong vision that proposes a future better than the status quo, the ability to articulate the vision, strong convictions in the vision, and the willingness to enact radical change.

We used to think that charismatic leaders were born. However, recent evidence suggests otherwise. Individuals can be trained to exhibit charismatic behaviors and can thus enjoy the benefits that accompany being labeled "a charismatic leader." Here are some specific charismatic behaviors you can engage in:

Project a powerful, confident, and dynamic presence.
Use a captivating and engaging voice tone. Convey
confidence. Talk directly to people, maintain direct eye
contact, and hold your body posture in a way that says
you're sure of yourself. Speak clearly, avoid stammering,
and avoid sprinkling your sentences with noncontent
phrases such as "uhhh" and "you know."

Articulate an overarching goal. Create a vision for the
future, specify unconventional ways of achieving the
vision, and communicate the vision to others. The road to
achieving the vision should be novel but appropriate to the
context. And remember that success is not only having a
vision but being able to get others to buy into it.

*Communicate high performance expectations and
confidence in others' ability to meet these expectations.*
State ambitious goals for individuals and groups and
demonstrate your belief that they will be achieved.

It's been shown that a person can learn to become
charismatic by following a three-step process. First, you need
to develop the aura of charisma by maintaining an optimistic
view, using passion as a catalyst for generating enthusiasm, and
communicating with the whole body, not just with words.
Second, you have to draw others in by creating a bond that
inspires others to follow. And third, you need to bring out the
potential in followers by tapping into their emotions. This
approach seems to work, as evidenced by success researchers
have had in actually scripting college students to "play"
charismatic. The students were taught to articulate an
overarching goal, to communicate high performance expec-

tations, to exhibit confidence in the ability of subordinates to meet those expectations, and to empathize with the needs of their subordinates. They learned to project a powerful, confident, and dynamic presence, and they practiced using a captivating and engaging voice tone. To further capture the dynamics and energy of charisma, the leaders were trained to evoke charismatic nonverbal characteristics: They alternated between pacing and sitting on the edges of their desks, leaned toward the subordinates, maintained direct eye contact, and had a relaxed posture and animated facial expressions. These researchers found that these students could learn how to project charisma. Moreover, subordinates of these leaders had higher task performance, task adjustment, and adjustment to the leader and to the group than did subordinates who worked under groups led by noncharismatic leaders.

> *Individuals can be trained to exhibit charismatic behaviors and can thus enjoy the benefits that accompany being labeled "a charismatic leader."*

What this tells us is that while some people clearly have an intuitive style that creates charisma, you can train yourself to exhibit charismatic behaviors. And to the degree to which you're successful, you will be perceived by others as a charismatic leader.

TRUTH 32

MAKE OTHERS DEPENDENT ON YOU

Effective leaders build a power base by making others dependent on them.

Power is the capacity for a leader to influence the behavior of another individual or group of individuals so that they'll do something they wouldn't otherwise do.

How do you make others dependent on you? There are two primary sources of power: your position in the organization and your personal characteristics.

In formal organizations, managerial positions come with authority—the right to give orders and expect the orders to be obeyed. In addition, a managerial position typically comes with the discretion to allocate rewards and enact punishments. Managers can give out desirable work assignments, appoint people to interesting or important projects, provide favorable performance reviews, and recommend salary increases. But they also can dish out undesirable work shifts and assignments, put people onto boring or low-profile projects, write up unfavorable appraisals, recommend undesirable transfers or even demotions, and limit merit raises.

You don't have to be a manager or have formal authority to have power. You can influence others through personal characteristics such as your expertise or personal charisma. In today's high-tech world, expertise has become an increasingly powerful source of influence. As jobs have become more specialized and complex, organizations and members have become dependent on experts with special skills or knowledge to achieve goals. Specialists such as software analysts, tax accountants, environmental engineers, and industrial psychologists are examples of individuals in organizations who can wield power as a result of their expertise. If you're director of human resources in your firm and you need valid selection tests to help you identify high-potential candidates—and you rely on the industrial psychologist on your staff to provide these valid tests—that industrial psychologist has expert power. Of course, charisma is also a powerful source of influence. If you possess charismatic traits, you can use this power to get others to do what you want.

The key to gaining power is making others dependent on you. And how do you do that? By gaining control over resources that are important and scarce.

If nobody wants what you've got, it's not going to create dependency. To create dependency, therefore, the thing(s) you control must be perceived as being important. It's been found, for instance, that organizations actively seek to avoid uncertainty. We should, therefore, expect that those individuals or groups who can reduce an organization's uncertainty will be perceived as controlling an important resource. For instance, during a labor strike, the organization's negotiating representatives have increased power. And engineers, as a group, are more powerful at Intel than at Procter & Gamble. An organization such as Intel, which is heavily technologically oriented, is highly dependent on its engineers to maintain its products' technical advantages and quality. And, at Intel, engineers are clearly a powerful group. At Procter & Gamble, marketing is the name of the game, and marketers are the most powerful occupational group. These examples support not only the view that the ability to reduce uncertainty increases a group's importance, and hence its power, but also the view that what's important

You don't have to be a manager or have formal authority to have power.

is situational. It varies among organizations and undoubtedly also varies over time within any given organization.

If something is plentiful, possession of it will not increase your power. A resource needs to be perceived as scarce to create dependency. This can help to explain how low-ranking members in an organization who have important knowledge not available to high-ranking members gain power over the high-ranking members. It also helps to make sense out of behaviors of low-ranking members that otherwise might seem illogical, such as destroying the procedure manuals that describe how a job is done, refusing to train people in their jobs or even to show others exactly what they do, creating specialized language and terminology that inhibit others from understanding their jobs, or operating in secrecy so an activity will appear more complex and difficult than it really is.

TRUTH 33

THERE'S NO IDEAL LEADERSHIP STYLE

It's tempting to look for a single leadership style that will work for you in any and all situations. Let me save you some time. Don't bother looking because there is no universal answer out there. Leadership styles have to be modified to reflect situational factors. Let's briefly describe the two most frequently used leadership styles, then we'll identify some situational variables you should consider in choosing between those styles.

Most leaders rely on either a directive or a supportive style. A directive leader lets employees know what is expected of them, schedules work to be done, and gives specific guidance as to how to accomplish tasks. A supportive leader is friendly and shows concern for the needs of employees.

Which one of these styles works best at any given time depends on characteristics of the employee (such as his or her experience and ability) and contextual factors in the workplace (such as the structure of jobs and the degree of work group support). Let me show you how you should modify your leadership style to reflect these situational factors.

Assume you've got an employee working for you who has lots of experience and strong abilities. You would err in using directive leadership with this person. In fact, she is likely to see this style as demeaning to her. She already knows her job; she doesn't need you to tell her how to do it. What she is likely to appreciate, however, is support and encouragement. Conversely, an employee who lacks experience or ability is likely to be frustrated by a friendly boss who provides only encouragement. What this employee wants is specific guidance and direction. When tasks are ambiguous, employees appreciate a manager who can provide directive leadership. But when employees' tasks are well structured, a supportive style works best. When there is substantial conflict within a work group, employees desire a directive leader. They want someone to lessen the conflict and make it easier for them to do their job.

Your job as a leader is to compensate for things lacking in your employee or the work setting.

There is no shortage of potential situational factors that can influence leadership style. In addition to those noted above, you should also consider things such as the quality of leader–employee relations, group norms, the organization's culture and leadership expectations, and how much power you have over employees regarding disciplining, promotions, pay increases, and the like. The key thing to keep in mind is that your job as a leader is to compensate for things lacking in your employee or the work setting. Your effectiveness as a leader will depend on how well you can identify those factors that are lacking and your ability to fill those gaps.

TRUTH 34

Adjust Your Leadership Style for Cultural Differences, or When in Rome . . .

Many managers fail as leaders because they forget to adjust their style for the cultural background of their employees. This applies to managers who take on assignments in a foreign country as well as managers who find themselves overseeing employees who come from a different cultural background.

National culture affects leadership style in two ways. It shapes the preferences of leaders; and it also defines what's acceptable to subordinates. Leaders can't choose their styles at will. They're constrained by the cultural conditions in which they have been socialized and that their subordinates have come to expect. For example, a manipulative or autocratic style is compatible with societies where there is a great deal of power inequality, and we find this in Arab and Latin American countries. Arab leaders are expected to be tough and strong. To show kindness or to be generous without being asked to do so is perceived as a sign of weakness. In Mexico, with its strong paternalistic tradition and the presence of the machismo principle, leaders are expected to be decisive and autocratic. Power inequality ratings should also be a good indicator of employee willingness to accept participative leadership.

Participation is likely to be most effective in countries that value equality, such as Norway, Finland, Denmark, and Sweden.

Leaders also need to take into consideration the expectations of their employees, even in their own countries, if those employees were raised in another culture. So a manager working in Los Angeles, who is overseeing a group of employees who were born and raised in Mexico, might be most effective if he biases his style toward being more autocratic because this is the style his employees are more used to in their homeland, may be closer to their expectations, and most likely to be associated by employees with effective leadership.

> *Most leadership theories have a U.S. bias.*

A final note on cultural differences. Remember that most leadership theories were developed in the United States, by Americans, with American subjects. That means they will have a U.S. bias. They emphasize follower responsibilities rather than rights; assume hedonism rather than commitment to duty or altruistic motivation; assume centrality of work and democratic value orientation; and stress rationality rather than spirituality, religion, or superstition. These assumptions don't apply universally. For instance, this doesn't describe India, which places a great deal more emphasis on spirituality. It doesn't describe Japan, where great concern is given toward ensuring that employees are able to "save face." And it doesn't apply in China, where it's acceptable to publicly humiliate employees.

Executives at the highly successful Asia Department Store in central China, as a case in point, who blatantly brag about practicing "heartless" management, require new employees to undergo two to four weeks of military training with units of the People's Liberation Army to increase their obedience, and conduct the store's in-house training sessions in a public place where employees can openly suffer embarrassment from their mistakes.

TRUTH 35

WHEN LEADERSHIP ISN'T IMPORTANT

Jim Collins, noted management expert and co-author of the best-selling book, *Built to Last*, has thrown some cold water on the leadership fire. "In the 1500s, people ascribed all events they didn't understand to God. Why did the crops fail? God. Why did someone die? God. Now our all-purpose explanation is leadership." Collins notes that when a company succeeds, people need someone to give the credit to. And that's typically the firm's CEO. Similarly, when the company does poorly, they need someone to blame. CEOs also play this role. But much of a company's success or failure is due to factors outside the influence of leadership. In many cases, success or failure is just a matter of being in the right or wrong place at a given time. Would Lou Gerstner, who is widely credited for IBM's successful turnaround in the 1990s, have been equally successful had he taken the head job at Burroughs instead? Not likely. IBM's product line, reputation, sales force, and other assets were better positioned to be improved than Burroughs.

When the demand for microchips was growing at 60 percent or more a year, leaders at microchip makers like Intel and Motorola were geniuses. Similarly, the CEOs at PC makers such as Compaq and Gateway were lauded in the 1990s, when demand for PCs was exploding. But by late 2000 and into 2001, these same leaders were being widely criticized for the decline in their company's business. And many CEOs were replaced as profits sank. The key leadership question would be: In a recession, when consumers and business are widely cutting back on technology purchases, how is firing a CEO going to increase the demand for chips and PCs? The answer, of course, is it can't.

Much of a company's success or failure is due to factors outside the influence of leadership.

The belief that some leadership style *will always* be effective *regardless* of the situation may not be true. Leadership may not always be important. Data from numerous studies collectively demonstrate that, in many situations, whatever actions leaders exhibit are irrelevant. Certain individual, job, and organizational variables can act as *substitutes* for leadership or *neutralize* the leader's effect to influence his or her followers.

Neutralizers make it impossible for leader behavior to make any difference to follower outcomes. They negate the leader's influence. Substitutes, on the other hand, make a leader's influence not only impossible but also unnecessary. They act as a replacement for the leader's influence. For example, characteristics of employees such as their experience, training, "professional" orientation, or indifference toward organizational rewards can substitute for, or neutralize the effect of, leadership. Experience and training, for instance, can replace the need for a leader's support or ability to create structure and reduce ambiguity. Jobs that are inherently unambiguous and routine or that are intrinsically satisfying may place fewer demands on the leadership variable. Organizational characteristics like explicit formalized goals, rigid rules and procedures, and cohesive work groups can replace formal leadership.

This recent recognition that leaders don't always have an impact on follower outcomes should not be that surprising. Yet supporters of the leadership concept have tended to place an undue burden on this variable for explaining and predicting behavior. It's too simplistic to consider employees as guided to goal accomplishments solely by the actions of their leader. It is important, therefore, to recognize explicitly that leadership is just another variable that influences employee performance.

PART IV

THE TRUTH
ABOUT
COMMUNICATION

TRUTH 36

HEARING ISN'T LISTENING

Many a manager hears very well but doesn't listen. Confused? Let me explain. Hearing is merely picking up sound vibrations. Listening is making sense out of what we hear. That is, listening requires paying attention, interpreting, and remembering sound stimuli.

Effective listening is active rather than passive. In passive listening, you're like a recorder. You absorb the information given. Active listening, in contrast, requires you to "get inside" the speaker's head so that you can understand the communication from his or her point of view. As an active listener, you try to understand what the speaker wants to communicate rather than what you want to understand. You also demonstrate acceptance of what is being said. You listen objectively without judging content. Finally, as an active listener, you take responsibility for completeness. You do whatever is necessary to get the fully intended meaning from the speaker's communication.

The following eight behaviors are associated with effective active-listening skills. If you want to improve your listening skills, look to these behaviors as guides:

1. *Make eye contact.* How do you feel when somebody doesn't look at you when you're speaking? If you're like most people, you're likely to interpret this behavior as aloofness or lack of interest.

2. *Exhibit affirmative head nods and appropriate facial expressions.* The effective listener shows interest in what is being said. How? Through nonverbal signals. Affirmative head nods and appropriate facial expressions, when added to good eye contact, convey to the speaker that you're listening.

3. *Avoid distracting actions or gestures.* The other side of showing interest is avoiding actions that suggest that your mind is somewhere else. When listening, don't look at your watch, shuffle papers, or engage in similar distractions. They make the speaker feel as if you're bored or uninterested and indicate that you aren't fully attentive.

> *Hearing is merely picking up sound vibrations. Listening is making sense out of what we hear.*

4. *Ask questions.* The critical listener analyzes what he or she hears and asks questions. This behavior provides clarification, ensures understanding, and assures the speaker that you're listening.

5. *Paraphrase.* Restate what the speaker has said in your own words. The active listener uses phrases such as "What

I hear you saying is . . ." or "Do you mean . . .?" By rephrasing what the speaker has said in your own words and feeding it back to the speaker, you verify the accuracy of your understanding.

6. *Avoid interrupting the speaker.* Let the speaker complete his or her thought before you try to respond. Don't try to second-guess where the speaker's thoughts are going. When the speaker is finished, you'll know it!

7. *Don't overtalk.* Although talking may be more fun and silence may be uncomfortable, you can't talk and listen at the same time. The active listener recognizes this fact and doesn't overtalk.

8. *Make smooth transitions between the roles of speaker and listener.* In most situations, you're continually shifting back and forth between the roles of speaker and listener. The active listener makes transitions smoothly from speaker to listener and back to speaker. From a listening perspective, this means concentrating on what a speaker has to say and avoiding thoughts about what you're going to say as soon as you get your chance.

TRUTH 37

CHOOSE THE RIGHT
COMMUNICATION CHANNEL

Neal L. Patterson, CEO at medical software maker Cerner Corp., likes e-mail. Maybe too much so. Upset with his staff's work ethic, he recently sent a seething e-mail to his firm's 400 managers. Here are some of that e-mail's highlights:

"Hell will freeze over before this CEO implements ANOTHER EMPLOYEE benefit in this culture . . . We are getting less than 40 hours of work from a large number of our Kansas City–based employees. The parking lot is sparsely used at 8 a.m.; likewise at 5 p.m. As managers—you either do not know what your EMPLOYEES are doing; or YOU do not CARE . . . You have a problem and you will fix it or I will replace you . . . What you are doing, as managers, with this company makes me SICK."

Patterson's e-mail additionally suggested that managers schedule meetings at 7 a.m., 6 p.m., and Saturday mornings; promised a staff reduction of 5 percent and institution of a time-clock system, and Patterson's intention to charge unapproved absences to employees' vacation time.

Within hours of this e-mail, copies of it had made its way onto a Yahoo! Web site. And within three days, Cerner's stock price had plummeted 22 percent. While one can argue about whether such harsh criticism should be communicated at all, one thing is certainly clear: Patterson erred by selecting the wrong channel for his message. Such an emotional and sensitive message would likely have been better received in a face-to-face meeting.

Why do people choose one channel of communication over another—for instance, a phone call instead of a face-to-face talk? And is there any general insight we might be able to provide regarding choice of communication channel?

Evidence indicates that channels differ in their capacity to convey information. Some are rich in that they have the ability to (1) handle multiple cues simultaneously, (2) facilitate rapid feedback, and (3) be very personal. Others are lean in that they score low on these three factors. For instance, face-to-face talk scores highest in channel richness because it provides for the maximum amount of information to be transmitted during a communication episode. That is, it offers multiple information cues (words, postures, facial expressions, gestures, intonations), immediate feedback (both verbal and nonverbal), and the personal touch of "being there." The telephone is another rich channel but less so than face-to-face communication. Impersonal written media such as bulletins and general reports rate low in richness. E-mail and memos fall somewhere in between.

The choice of one channel over another should be determined by whether the message is routine or nonroutine. The former types of messages tend to be straightforward and have a minimum of ambiguity. The latter are likely to be

ack mechanism by highlighting issues that
der relevant. For instance, the grapevine can
ncerns. If the grapevine is carrying a rumor of
nd if you know the rumor is totally false, the
s meaning. It reflects the fears and concerns of
, hence, should not be ignored. Importantly,
actually manage the grapevine by planting
it wants employees to hear. Managers should
ine patterns and observe which individuals are
what issues and who is likely to actively pass
In addition, managers need to reduce the
equences that rumors can create. If you come
ive rumor and think it has the potential to be
consider how you might lessen its impact by
ganizational communication. This could include
timetables for making important decisions;
cisions and behaviors that may appear inconsistent
emphasizing the downside, as well as the upside,
ecisions and future plans; and openly discussing
possibilities.

complicated and have the potential for misunderstanding. Managers can communicate routine messages efficiently through channels that are lower in richness. However, they can communicate nonroutine messages effectively only by selecting rich channels.

Evidence indicates that high-performing managers tend to be more media sensitive than low-performing managers. That is, they're better able to match appropriate media richness with the ambiguity involved in the communication.

Findings on media richness are consistent with organizational trends and practices during the past decade. It's not just coincidence that more and more senior managers have been using meetings to facilitate communication and regularly leaving the isolated sanctuary of their executive offices to manage-by-walking-around. These executives are relying on richer channels of communication to transmit the more ambiguous messages they need to convey. The past decade has been characterized

High-performing managers tend to be more media sensitive than low-performing managers.

by organizations closing facilities, imposing large layoffs, restructuring, merging, consolidating, and introducing new products and services at an accelerated pace—all nonroutine messages high in ambiguity and requiring the use of channels that can convey a large amount of information. It's not surprising, therefore, to see the most effective managers expanding their use of rich channels.

TRUTH 38

LISTEN TO THE GRAPEVINE

In the fall of 2000, the rumor mill was especially active at Coca-Cola's Atlanta headquarters. The company was in the midst of a major reorganization that had included 5,200 layoffs worldwide earlier in the year. Rumors were saying that key executives were leaving, that there were ongoing turf wars among senior executives, and that more layoffs were pending. These rumors were beginning to seriously undermine morale at Coke. In an attempt to shut down the rumor mill, James Chestnut, the company's executive vice president, tried to set things straight. He acknowledged that the company's senior management hadn't done a good enough job of telling employees about the changes that were taking place. He pledged "better and more frequent communication."

As executives at Coke have learned, rumors can be a major distraction for employees. This doesn't mean that management can ever eliminate the grapevine. But certain conditions tend to stimulate grapevine activity. And importantly, as executives at Coke did, management needs to monitor the grapevine and respond to the issues with which it's concerned.

Rumors in
They structure
or fragmented in
group members i
("I'm an insider a
to make you an i

Studies have
situations that are
and under conditi
frequently contain
rumors flourish
izations. The sec
competition that typ
vail in large organi
around issues such as
ment of new bosses, r
of offices, realignment
assignments, and la
create conditions that
age and sustain rumors
grapevine.

Realize that the gra
isn't going to go away. I
important part of any gro
organization's communic.
system. Astute managers
cept the existence of the gr
They use it to identify issues
and that are likely to creat

filter and feedb
employees cons
tap employee c
a mass layoff, a
message still ha
employees and
managers can
messages that
monitor grape
interested in
rumors along
negative cons
across an ac
destructive,
improving or
announcing
explaining de
or secretive;
of current
worst-case

TRUTH 39

MEN AND WOMEN
DO COMMUNICATE DIFFERENTLY

Recent research confirms what many of us have thought true since our adolescent days: Men and women often have difficulty communicating with each other. The reason? They use conversation for different purposes. Men tend to use talk to emphasize status, while women generally use it to create connection. These differences create real challenges for managers.

Communication is a continual balancing act, juggling the conflicting needs for intimacy and independence. Intimacy emphasizes closeness and commonalties. Independence emphasizes separateness and differences. But men and women handle these conflicts differently. Women speak and hear a language of connection and intimacy, while men speak and hear a language of status, power, and independence. So, for many men, conversations are primarily a means to preserve independence and maintain status in a hierarchical social order. For many women, conversations are negotiations for closeness in which people try to seek and give confirmation and support. Here are some examples.

Men frequently complain that women ramble on and on about their problems. Women criticize men for not listening. What's happening is that when men hear a problem, they frequently assert their desire for independence and control by offering solutions. Many women, on the other hand, view telling a problem as a means to promote closeness. The women present the problem to gain support and connection, not to get the man's advice. Mutual understanding is symmetrical; but giving advice is asymmetrical—it sets up the advice giver as more knowledgeable and more in control. This contributes to distancing men and women in their efforts to communicate.

Men are often more direct than women in conversation. A man might say, "I think you're wrong on that point." A woman might say, "Have you looked at the marketing department's research report on that point?" (the implication being that the report will show the error). Men frequently see female indirectness as "covert" or "sneaky," but women are not as concerned as men with the status and one-upmanship that directness often creates.

> *Men tend to use talk to emphasize status, while women generally use it to create connection.*

Women tend to be less boastful than men. They often downplay their authority or accomplishments to avoid appearing as braggarts and to take the other person's feelings into account. However, men can frequently misinterpret this and incorrectly conclude that a woman is less confident and competent than she really is.

Men often criticize women for seeming to apologize all the time. For instance, men tend to see the phrase "I'm sorry" as a weakness because they interpret the phrase to mean the woman is accepting blame, when he knows she's not to blame. The woman also knows she's not to blame. The problem is that women frequently use "I'm sorry" to express regret and restore balance to a conversation: "I know you must feel badly about this; I do, too." For many women, "I'm sorry" is an expression of understanding and caring about the other person's feelings rather than an apology.

TRUTH 40

WHAT YOU DO OVERPOWERS
WHAT YOU SAY

It's not what you say, it's what you do! Actions DO speak louder than words.

When faced with inconsistencies between words and actions, people tend to give greater credence to actions. It's behavior that counts!

The implication of this for managers is: You're a role model. Employees will imitate your behavior and attitudes. They watch what their boss does and then imitate or adapt accordingly. This doesn't mean, however, that words fall on deaf ears. Words can influence others. But when words and actions diverge, people focus most on what they see in terms of behavior.

To illustrate, consider your attitude toward employees and your ethical behavior. Many a manager will pontificate on the importance of his or her employees: "It's people that make the difference here" or "People are our most important asset." Then they engage in practices that contradict this attitude. For instance, they don't listen to employees' complaints, they're insensitive to employee personal problems, or they let good people leave for other jobs without making a concerted effort to keep them. When employees see such contradictions, they're most likely to believe the *actions* of managers regardless of what they hear those managers say. Similarly, managers who want to establish a strong ethical climate in their workplaces need to make sure their deeds match their words. Talk about high standards of integrity will fall on deaf ears if they're uttered by managers who pad their expense account, take office supplies home for personal use, or regularly come in late to work or leave early.

Contradictions between words and actions can be most damaging to a manager's attempt to build trust with his or her employees. A manager

Actions DO speak louder than words.

who is trusted is one who can be depended upon to not take advantage of people or situations. It's hard for employees to trust a manager who says one thing but does another.

There is an obvious exception to the previous findings. An increasing number of leaders have developed the skill of shaping words and putting the proper "spin" on situations so that others focus on the leader's words rather than the behavior. Successful politicians seem particularly adept at this skill. Why people believe these spins when faced with conflicting behavioral evidence is not clear. But it certainly underscores the power of words to shape people's opinions. Do we want to believe that our leaders would not lie to us? Do we want to believe what politicians say, especially when we hold them in high regard? Do we give high-status people, for whom we've previously given our vote, the benefit of the doubt when confronted with their negative behavior? These are questions that, at least at this time, we don't have answers to.

TRUTH 41

THE CASE FOR
OPEN-BOOK MANAGEMENT

An increasing number of companies are redefining their organization's culture around open communications. In contrast to the historical notion that financial details were something left to management, companies like Springfield Remanufacturing, Allstate Insurance, Rhino Foods, Patagonia, and Sprint are opening their books and explaining financial details to employees. Open-book management (OBM) discards the notion that bosses run things and employees do what they're told. Instead, it allows every employee to think and behave like an owner. Access to detailed financial information, and the ability to understand that information, makes employees think like owners. And this leads to them making decisions that are best for the organization, not just for themselves. Employees solve problems, help cut costs, reduce defects, and do what's necessary to give the customer better service.

There are three key elements to any OBM program. First, management opens the company's books and shares detailed financial and operating information with employees. The logic here is if employees don't know how the company makes money, how can they be expected to make the firm more successful? Second, employees need to be taught to understand the company's financial statements. This means management must provide employees with a basic course in how to read and interpret income statements, balance sheets, and cash flow statements. And third, management needs to show employees how their work influences financial results. Showing employees the impact of their jobs on the bottom line makes financial statement analysis relevant.

Does it work? Most firms that have introduced OBM offer evidence that it has significantly helped the business. For instance, Springfield Remanufacturing was losing $61,000 on sales of $16 million. Then it instituted OBM. Management attributes much of the company's current success—profits of $6 million a year on sales of $100 million—to OBM. Similarly, Allstate's Business Insurance Group used OBM to boost return on equity from 2.9 percent to 16.5 percent in just three years.

OBM allows every employee to think and behave like an owner.

Does OBM always work? No. There have been cases where employees have misused and misinterpreted the information they got from management. And some firms have found that OBM resulted in confidential information being leaked to competitors.

When OBM succeeds, two factors seem to exist. First, the organization or unit where it's implemented tends to be small. It's a lot easier to introduce OBM in a small, start-up company than in a large, geographically dispersed company that has operated for years with closed books and little employee involvement. Second, there needs to be a mutually trusting relationship between management and workers. In organizational cultures where management doesn't trust employees to act responsibly or where managers and accountants have been trained to keep information under lock and key, OBM isn't likely to work. Nor will it succeed where employees believe any new change program is only likely to further manipulate or exploit them for management's advantage.

PART V

THE TRUTH ABOUT BUILDING TEAMS

TRUTH 42

WHAT WE KNOW
THAT MAKES TEAMS WORK

Teams are hot! They have become an essential device for structuring job activities. But how do managers create effective teams?

The key components making up effective teams can be subsumed into four general categories. The first category is *work design*. The second relates to the team's *composition*. Third are the resources and other *contextual* influences that make teams effective. Finally, *process* variables reflect the things that go on in the team that influence effectiveness.

Work Design

Teams work best when employees have freedom and autonomy, the opportunity to utilize different skills and talents, the ability to complete a whole and identifiable task or product, and a task or project that has a substantial impact on others. The evidence indicates that these characteristics enhance member motivation and increase team effectiveness because they increase members' sense of responsibility and ownership over the work and because they make the work more interesting to perform.

complicated and have the potential for misunderstanding. Managers can communicate routine messages efficiently through channels that are lower in richness. However, they can communicate nonroutine messages effectively only by selecting rich channels.

Evidence indicates that high-performing managers tend to be more media sensitive than low-performing managers. That is, they're better able to match appropriate media richness with the ambiguity involved in the communication.

Findings on media richness are consistent with organizational trends and practices during the past decade. It's not just coincidence that more and more senior managers have been using meetings to facilitate communication and regularly leaving the isolated sanctuary of their executive offices to manage-by-walking-around. These executives are relying on richer channels of communication to transmit the more ambiguous messages they need to convey. The past decade has been characterized

High-performing managers tend to be more media sensitive than low-performing managers.

by organizations closing facilities, imposing large layoffs, restructuring, merging, consolidating, and introducing new products and services at an accelerated pace—all nonroutine messages high in ambiguity and requiring the use of channels that can convey a large amount of information. It's not surprising, therefore, to see the most effective managers expanding their use of rich channels.

TRUTH 38

LISTEN TO THE GRAPEVINE

In the fall of 2000, the rumor mill was especially active at Coca-Cola's Atlanta headquarters. The company was in the midst of a major reorganization that had included 5,200 layoffs worldwide earlier in the year. Rumors were saying that key executives were leaving, that there were ongoing turf wars among senior executives, and that more layoffs were pending. These rumors were beginning to seriously undermine morale at Coke. In an attempt to shut down the rumor mill, James Chestnut, the company's executive vice president, tried to set things straight. He acknowledged that the company's senior management hadn't done a good enough job of telling employees about the changes that were taking place. He pledged "better and more frequent communication."

As executives at Coke have learned, rumors can be a major distraction for employees. This doesn't mean that management can ever eliminate the grapevine. But certain conditions tend to stimulate grapevine activity. And importantly, as executives at Coke did, management needs to monitor the grapevine and respond to the issues with which it's concerned.

Rumors in the workplace perform a number of purposes. They structure and reduce anxiety. They make sense of limited or fragmented information. They serve as a vehicle to organize group members into coalitions. And they signal a sender's status ("I'm an insider and you're not!") or power ("I have the power to make you an insider.")

Studies have found that rumors emerge as a response to situations that are important to us, where there is ambiguity, and under conditions that arouse anxiety. Work situations frequently contain these three elements, which explains why rumors flourish in organizations. The secrecy and competition that typically prevail in large organizations— around issues such as appointment of new bosses, relocation of offices, realignment of work assignments, and layoffs— create conditions that encourage and sustain rumors on the grapevine.

Rumors emerge as a response to situations that are important to us, where there is ambiguity, and under conditions that arouse anxiety.

Realize that the grapevine isn't going to go away. It's an important part of any group or organization's communication system. Astute managers accept the existence of the grapevine and use it in beneficial ways. They use it to identify issues that employees consider important and that are likely to create anxiety. They view it as both a filter and feedback mechanism by highlighting issues that employees consider relevant. For instance, the grapevine can tap employee concerns. If the grapevine is carrying a rumor of a mass layoff, and if you know the rumor is totally false, the message still has meaning. It reflects the fears and concerns of employees and, hence, should not be ignored. Importantly, managers can actually manage the grapevine by planting messages that it wants employees to hear. Managers should monitor grapevine patterns and observe which individuals are interested in what issues and who is likely to actively pass rumors along. In addition, managers need to reduce the negative consequences that rumors can create. If you come across an active rumor and think it has the potential to be destructive, consider how you might lessen its impact by improving organizational communication. This could include announcing timetables for making important decisions; explaining decisions and behaviors that may appear inconsistent or secretive; emphasizing the downside, as well as the upside, of current decisions and future plans; and openly discussing worst-case possibilities.

TRUTH 39

MEN AND WOMEN
DO COMMUNICATE DIFFERENTLY

Recent research confirms what many of us have thought true since our adolescent days: Men and women often have difficulty communicating with each other. The reason? They use conversation for different purposes. Men tend to use talk to emphasize status, while women generally use it to create connection. These differences create real challenges for managers.

Communication is a continual balancing act, juggling the conflicting needs for intimacy and independence. Intimacy emphasizes closeness and commonalties. Independence emphasizes separateness and differences. But men and women handle these conflicts differently. Women speak and hear a language of connection and intimacy, while men speak and hear a language of status, power, and independence. So, for many men, conversations are primarily a means to preserve independence and maintain status in a hierarchical social order. For many women, conversations are negotiations for closeness in which people try to seek and give confirmation and support. Here are some examples.

Men frequently complain that women ramble on and on about their problems. Women criticize men for not listening. What's happening is that when men hear a problem, they frequently assert their desire for independence and control by offering solutions. Many women, on the other hand, view telling a problem as a means to promote closeness. The women present the problem to gain support and connection, not to get the man's advice. Mutual understanding is symmetrical; but giving advice is asymmetrical—it sets up the advice giver as more knowledgeable and more in control. This contributes to distancing men and women in their efforts to communicate.

Men are often more direct than women in conversation. A man might say, "I think you're wrong on that point." A woman might say, "Have you looked at the marketing department's research report on that point?" (the implication being that the report will show the error). Men frequently see female indirectness as "covert" or "sneaky," but women are not as concerned as men with the status and one-upmanship that directness often creates.

> *Men tend to use talk to emphasize status, while women generally use it to create connection.*

Women tend to be less boastful than men. They often downplay their authority or accomplishments to avoid appearing as braggarts and to take the other person's feelings into account. However, men can frequently misinterpret this

and incorrectly conclude that a woman is less confident and competent than she really is.

Men often criticize women for seeming to apologize all the time. For instance, men tend to see the phrase "I'm sorry" as a weakness because they interpret the phrase to mean the woman is accepting blame, when he knows she's not to blame. The woman also knows she's not to blame. The problem is that women frequently use "I'm sorry" to express regret and restore balance to a conversation: "I know you must feel badly about this; I do, too." For many women, "I'm sorry" is an expression of understanding and caring about the other person's feelings rather than an apology.

TRUTH 40

WHAT YOU DO OVERPOWERS
WHAT YOU SAY

It's not what you say, it's what you do! Actions DO speak louder than words.

When faced with inconsistencies between words and actions, people tend to give greater credence to actions. It's behavior that counts!

The implication of this for managers is: You're a role model. Employees will imitate your behavior and attitudes. They watch what their boss does and then imitate or adapt accordingly. This doesn't mean, however, that words fall on deaf ears. Words can influence others. But when words and actions diverge, people focus most on what they see in terms of behavior.

To illustrate, consider your attitude toward employees and your ethical behavior. Many a manager will pontificate on the importance of his or her employees: "It's people that make the difference here" or "People are our most important asset." Then they engage in practices that contradict this attitude. For instance, they don't listen to employees' complaints, they're insensitive to employee personal problems, or they let good people leave for other jobs without making a concerted effort to

keep them. When employees see such contradictions, they're most likely to believe the *actions* of managers regardless of what they hear those managers say. Similarly, managers who want to establish a strong ethical climate in their workplaces need to make sure their deeds match their words. Talk about high standards of integrity will fall on deaf ears if they're uttered by managers who pad their expense account, take office supplies home for personal use, or regularly come in late to work or leave early.

Contradictions between words and actions can be most damaging to a manager's attempt to build trust with his or her employees. A manager

Actions DO speak louder than words.

who is trusted is one who can be depended upon to not take advantage of people or situations. It's hard for employees to trust a manager who says one thing but does another.

There is an obvious exception to the previous findings. An increasing number of leaders have developed the skill of shaping words and putting the proper "spin" on situations so that others focus on the leader's words rather than the behavior. Successful politicians seem particularly adept at this skill. Why people believe these spins when faced with conflicting behavioral evidence is not clear. But it certainly underscores the power of words to shape people's opinions. Do we want to believe that our leaders would not lie to us? Do we want to believe what politicians say, especially when we hold them in high regard? Do we give high-status people, for whom we've previously given our vote, the benefit of the doubt when confronted with their negative behavior? These are questions that, at least at this time, we don't have answers to.

TRUTH 41

THE CASE FOR
OPEN-BOOK MANAGEMENT

An increasing number of companies are redefining their organization's culture around open communications. In contrast to the historical notion that financial details were something left to management, companies like Springfield Remanufacturing, Allstate Insurance, Rhino Foods, Patagonia, and Sprint are opening their books and explaining financial details to employees. Open-book management (OBM) discards the notion that bosses run things and employees do what they're told. Instead, it allows every employee to think and behave like an owner. Access to detailed financial information, and the ability to understand that information, makes employees think like owners. And this leads to them making decisions that are best for the organization, not just for themselves. Employees solve problems, help cut costs, reduce defects, and do what's necessary to give the customer better service.

There are three key elements to any OBM program. First, management opens the company's books and shares detailed financial and operating information with employees. The logic here is if employees don't know how the company makes

money, how can they be expected to make the firm more successful? Second, employees need to be taught to understand the company's financial statements. This means management must provide employees with a basic course in how to read and interpret income statements, balance sheets, and cash flow statements. And third, management needs to show employees how their work influences financial results. Showing employees the impact of their jobs on the bottom line makes financial statement analysis relevant.

Does it work? Most firms that have introduced OBM offer evidence that it has significantly helped the business. For instance, Springfield Remanufacturing was losing $61,000 on sales of $16 million. Then it instituted OBM. Management attributes much of the company's current success—profits of $6 million a year on sales of $100 million—to OBM. Similarly, Allstate's Business Insurance Group used OBM to boost return on equity from 2.9 percent to 16.5 percent in just three years.

OBM allows every employee to think and behave like an owner.

Does OBM always work? No. There have been cases where employees have misused and misinterpreted the information they got from management. And some firms have found that OBM resulted in confidential information being leaked to competitors.

When OBM succeeds, two factors seem to exist. First, the organization or unit where it's implemented tends to be

small. It's a lot easier to introduce OBM in a small, start-up company than in a large, geographically dispersed company that has operated for years with closed books and little employee involvement. Second, there needs to be a mutually trusting relationship between management and workers. In organizational cultures where management doesn't trust employees to act responsibly or where managers and accountants have been trained to keep information under lock and key, OBM isn't likely to work. Nor will it succeed where employees believe any new change program is only likely to further manipulate or exploit them for management's advantage.

PART V

THE TRUTH ABOUT BUILDING TEAMS

TRUTH **42**

Teams are hot! They have become an essential device for structuring job activities. But how do managers create effective teams?

The key components making up effective teams can be subsumed into four general categories. The first category is *work design*. The second relates to the team's *composition*. Third are the resources and other *contextual* influences that make teams effective. Finally, *process* variables reflect the things that go on in the team that influence effectiveness.

Work Design

Teams work best when employees have freedom and autonomy, the opportunity to utilize different skills and talents, the ability to complete a whole and identifiable task or product, and a task or project that has a substantial impact on others. The evidence indicates that these characteristics enhance member motivation and increase team effectiveness because they increase members' sense of responsibility and ownership over the work and because they make the work more interesting to perform.

Composition

This category includes variables that relate to how teams should be staffed: the ability and personality of team members, size of the team, member flexibility, and members' preference for teamwork.

To perform effectively, a team requires three different types of skills. First, it needs people with *technical expertise*. Second, it needs people with the *problem-solving and decision-making skills* to be able to identify problems, generate alternatives, evaluate those alternatives, and make competent choices. Finally, teams need people with good listening, feedback, conflict resolution, and other *interpersonal skills*. No team can achieve its full performance potential without developing all three types of skills.

Personality has a significant influence on team behavior. Specifically, teams that rate higher in average levels of extraversion, agreeableness, conscientiousness, and emotional stability tend to receive higher managerial ratings for team performance.

The most effective teams are neither very small (under 4 or 5) or very large (over a dozen). Very small teams are likely to lack for diversity of views and teams of more than 12 have difficulty getting much done. If a natural work unit is larger than 12 and you want a team effort, consider breaking the group into subteams.

Teams made up of flexible individuals have members who can complete each other's tasks. This is an obvious plus to a team because it greatly improves its adaptability and makes it less reliant on any single member. So selecting members who themselves value flexibility, then cross-training them to be able to do each other's jobs, should lead to higher team performance over time.

Not every employee is a team player. When people who would prefer to work alone are required to team up, there is a direct threat to the team's morale. This suggests that, when selecting team members, individual preferences be considered as well as abilities, personalities, and skills.

Context

The three contextual factors that appear to be most significantly related to team performance are the presence of adequate resources, effective leadership, and a performance evaluation and reward system that reflects team contributions.

Teams have become an essential device for structuring job activities.

Work groups are part of a larger organization system. As such, all work teams rely on resources outside the group to sustain it. And a scarcity of resources directly reduces the ability of the team to perform its job effectively. Supportive resources include timely information, equipment, adequate staffing, encouragement, and administrative assistance.

Team members must agree on who is to do what and ensure that all members contribute equally in sharing the workload. In addition, the team needs to determine how schedules will be set, what skills need to be developed, how the group will resolve conflicts, and how the group will make and modify decisions. Agreeing on the specifics of work and how they fit together to integrate individual skills requires team leadership and structure.

How do you get team members to be both individually and jointly accountable? The traditional, individually oriented evaluation and reward system needs to be modified to reflect team performance. In addition to evaluating and rewarding employees for their individual contributions, management should consider group-based appraisals, profit sharing, gain sharing, small-group incentives, and other system modifications that will reinforce team effort and commitment.

Process

The final category related to team effectiveness is process variables. These include member commitment to a common purpose, establishment of specific team goals, and a managed level of conflict.

Effective teams have a common and meaningful purpose that provides direction, momentum, and commitment for members. Members of successful teams put a tremendous amount of time and effort into discussing, shaping, and agreeing upon a purpose that belongs to them both collectively and individually.

Successful teams translate their common purpose into specific, measurable, and realistic performance goals. These goals help teams maintain their focus on getting results.

Conflict on a team isn't necessarily bad. Teams that are devoid of conflict are likely to become apathetic and stagnant. Conflict can improve team effectiveness when it stimulates discussion, promotes critical assessment of problems and options, and leads to better team decisions.

TRUTH 43

2 + 2 Doesn't Necessarily Equal 4

Proponents of teams frequently say that one of the reasons business firms should organize around teams is that they create *positive* synergy. That is, the productivity output of a team is greater than would occur if individual members had worked alone because the sense of team spirit spurs individual effort. So 2 + 2 can equal 5. The truth is that teams often create *negative* synergy. Individuals expend less effort when working collectively than when working individually, so 2 + 2 can equal 3! The reason for this negative outcome? It's called social loafing.

In the late 1920s, a German psychologist named Max Ringelmann compared the results of individual and group performance on a rope-pulling task. He expected that the group's effort would be equal to the sum of the efforts of individuals within the group. For instance, three people pulling together should exert three times as much pull on the rope as one person, and eight people should exert eight times as much pull. Ringelmann's results, however, didn't confirm his expectations. Groups of three people exerted a force only two-

and-a-half times the average individual performance. Groups of eight collectively achieved less than four times the solo rate.

Replications of Ringelmann's research with similar tasks have generally supported his findings. Increases in group size are inversely related to individual performance. More may be better in the sense that the total productivity of a group of four is greater than that of one or two people, but the individual productivity of each group member declines.

What causes this social loafing effect? It may be due to a belief that others in the group are not carrying their fair share. If you see others as lazy or inept, you can re-establish equity by reducing your effort. Another explanation is dispersion of responsibility. Because the results of the group cannot be attributed to any single person, the relationship between an individual's input and the group's output is clouded. In such situations, individuals may be tempted to become "free riders" and coast on the group's efforts. In other words, there will be a reduction in efficiency where individuals think that their contribution cannot be measured.

The truth is that teams often create negative synergy.

What are the implications of social loafing for the design of work teams? Where you use teams to enhance morale or improve coordination, you need to also provide means for identifying and measuring individual efforts. If this isn't done, you have to weigh the potential losses in productivity from using groups against any possible gains in worker satisfaction.

TRUTH **44**

WE'RE NOT ALL EQUAL:
STATUS MATTERS!

M any of us like to think that status isn't as important as it was a generation or two ago. We can point to the hippie movement, equal rights legislation, and the recent rapid growth of small entrepreneurial firms as forces that have made organizations more egalitarian. The reality is that we continue to live in an essentially class-structured society.

Despite all attempts to make it more egalitarian, we have made little progress toward a classless society. Even the smallest group will develop roles and rituals to differentiate its members. And we're finding that even the New Economy organizations adapt mechanisms to create status differences. Take, for instance, e-mail. Here is a communication device that was touted as being able to democratize organizations. It allows people to communicate up and down hierarchical lines, unimpeded by gatekeepers and protocols. But you know what? Status differences have creeped into the e-mail process. A recent study of some 30,000 e-mail messages at a New Economy firm that didn't use job titles, was organized around teams, and prided itself on democratic decision making provides interesting insights. People had found ways to create social distinctions. High-status employees tended to send short, curt messages, in part to minimize contact with lower-status workers but also to convey comfort with their own authority. In contrast, mid-status employees tended to produce long, argumentative messages loaded with jargon or overexplained answers to simple questions. And low-status employees' e-mails would contain non–work-related elements like forwarded jokes or happy-face "emoticons." In addition, the study found that senior managers would take the longest to reply, had the poorest spelling, and the worst grammar—which all conveyed that they have better things to do with their time.

Even the smallest group will develop roles and rituals to differentiate its members.

Status is an important factor in understanding human behavior because it is a significant motivator and can create major problems when people perceive status inequities. A fancy title, a large office, or even an impressive business card can carry a lot of weight in motivating employees. Conversely, a lack of status accoutrements can make people feel less important. Status inequities create frustration and can adversely influence employee performance and even lead to an unwanted resignation.

Keep in mind that the criteria that create status differ widely between cultures. For instance, status for Latin Americans and Asians tends to be derived from family position and formal roles held in organizations. In contrast, status in countries like the United States and Australia tends to be bestowed more on accomplishments than titles and family trees. The message here is to make sure you understand who and what holds status when interacting with people from a different culture than your own. An American manager who doesn't understand that office size is no measure of a Japanese executive's position or who fails to grasp the importance that the British place on family geneology and social class is likely to unintentionally offend his Japanese or British counterpart and, in so doing, lessen his interpersonal effectiveness.

TRUTH 45

NOT EVERYONE IS TEAM MATERIAL

Many people are not inherently team players. They are loners or people who want to be recognized for their individual achievements. There are also a great many organizations that have historically nurtured individual accomplishments. They have created competitive work environments where only the strong survive. If these organizations adopt teams, what can they do about the "I have to look out for me" employees that they created? And finally, countries differ in terms of their "groupiness." What if an organization wants to introduce teams into a work population that is made up largely of individuals born and raised in a highly individualistic society? As one writer so aptly put it, in describing the role of teams in the United States: "Americans don't grow up learning how to function in teams. In school we never receive a team report card or learn the names of the team of sailors who traveled with Columbus to America." This limitation would obviously be just as true of Canadians, Britons, Australians, and others from highly individualistic societies.

The previous points are meant to dramatize that one substantial barrier to using work teams is individual resistance. An employee's success is no longer defined in terms of individual performance. To perform well as team members, individuals must be able to communicate openly and honestly; to confront differences and resolve conflicts; and to sublimate personal goals for the good of the team. For many employees, these are difficult—sometimes impossible—tasks. The challenge of creating team players will be greatest where (1) the national culture is highly individualistic and (2) the teams are being introduced into an established organization that has historically valued individual achievement. These conditions describe, for instance, what faced managers at AT&T, Ford, Motorola, and other large U.S.–based companies. These firms prospered by hiring and rewarding corporate stars; they created a competitive climate that encouraged individual achievement and recognition. Employees in these types of firms can be jolted by a sudden shift to the importance of team play. One veteran employee of a large company, who had done very well by working alone,

To perform well as team members, individuals must be able to communicate openly and honestly; to confront differences and resolve conflicts; and to sublimate personal goals for the good of the team.

described the experience of joining a team: "I'm learning my lesson. I just had my first negative performance appraisal in 20 years."

On the other hand, the challenge for management is less demanding when teams are introduced where employees have strong "group" values—such as in Japan or Mexico—or in new organizations that use teams as their initial form for structuring work. Mercedes-Benz's new plant in Alabama, for instance, was designed around teams from its inception. Everyone at the plant was initially hired with the knowledge that they would be working in teams. And the ability to be a good team player was a basic hiring qualification that all new employees had to meet.

The following summarizes the primary options managers have for trying to turn individuals into team players.

Selection. Some people already possess the interpersonal skills to be effective team players. When hiring team members, in addition to the technical skills required to fill the job, care should be taken to ensure that candidates can fulfill their team roles as well as technical requirements.

Training. A large proportion of people raised on the importance of individual accomplishment can be trained to become team players. Training specialists conduct exercises that allow employees to experience the satisfaction that teamwork can provide. They typically offer workshops to help employees improve their problem-solving, communication, negotiation, conflict-management, and coaching skills.

Rewards. The reward system needs to be reworked to encourage cooperative efforts rather than competitive ones. Promotions, pay raises, and other forms of recognition should be given to individuals for how effective they are as a collaborative team member.

Unfortunately, in organizations that are undergoing the transformation to teams, there will likely be some current employees who will resist team training or prove untrainable. Your options with such individuals are essentially two. You can transfer them to another unit within the organization that does not have teams, if this possibility exists. The other choice is obvious and acknowledges that some employees may become casualties of the team approach.

PART VI

THE TRUTH
ABOUT MANAGING
CONFLICTS

TRUTH 46

THE CASE FOR CONFLICT

In our discussion of effective teams, we said that conflict isn't necessarily bad. Research tells us that there are three types of conflict: task, relationship, and process. Task conflict relates to the content and goals of the work. Relationship conflict focuses on interpersonal relationships. And process conflict relates to how work gets done. The evidence indicates that while relationship conflicts are almost always dysfunctional in groups or organizations, low levels of process and task conflict are often functional. Since many people seem to have difficulty with thinking of conflict in positive terms, let me make the argument to support the constructive side of conflict.

Conflict is constructive when it improves the quality of decisions, stimulates creativity and innovation, encourages interest and curiosity among group members, provides the medium through which problems can be aired and tensions released, and fosters an environment of self-evaluation and change. The evidence suggests that conflict can improve the quality of decision making by allowing all points, particularly the ones that are unusual or held by a minority, to be weighed in important decisions. Conflict is an antidote for groups that might be tempted to "rubber stamp" decisions that are based on weak assumptions, inadequate consideration of relevant alternatives, or other debilities. Conflict challenges the status quo and therefore furthers the creation of new ideas, promotes reassessment of group goals and activities, and increases the probability that a group will respond to change.

For an example of a company that has suffered because it has had too little functional conflict, you don't have to look further than automobile behemoth General Motors. Many of GM's problems over the past three decades can be traced to a lack of functional conflict. It hired and promoted individuals who were "yes men," loyal to GM to the point of never questioning company actions. Managers were, for the most part, conservative white Anglo-Saxon males raised in the midwestern United States and who resisted change—they preferred looking back to past successes rather than forward to new challenges. They were almost sanctimonious in their belief that what had worked in the past would continue to work in the future. Moreover, by sheltering executives in the company's Detroit offices and encouraging them to socialize with others inside the GM ranks, the company further insulated managers from conflicting perspectives.

There is substantial evidence indicating that conflict can be positively related to productivity. For instance, it was demonstrated that, among established groups, performance tended to improve more when there was conflict among members than when there was fairly close agreement. The investigators observed that when groups analyzed decisions that had been made by the individual members of that group, the average improvement among the high-conflict groups was

73 percent greater than that of those groups characterized by low-conflict conditions. Others have found similar results: Groups composed of members with different interests tend to produce higher-quality solutions to a variety of problems than do homogeneous groups.

Evidence demonstrates that cultural diversity among group and organization members can increase creativity, improve the quality of decisions, and facilitate change by enhancing member flexibility. For example, researchers compared decision-making groups composed of all-Anglo individuals with groups that also contained members from Asian, Hispanic, and black ethnic groups. The ethnically diverse groups produced more effective and more feasible ideas and the unique ideas they generated tended to be of higher quality than the unique ideas produced by the all-Anglo group.

Many of General Motors' problems over the past three decades can be traced to a lack of functional conflict.

Similarly, studies of systems analysts and research and development scientists support the constructive value of conflict. An investigation of 22 teams of systems analysts found that the more incompatible groups were likely to be more productive. Research and development scientists have been found to be most productive where there is a certain amount of intellectual conflict.

TRUTH 47

POOR COMMUNICATION ISN'T THE SOURCE OF MOST CONFLICTS

W hen I ask people the primary source of their work-related conflicts, the most frequent answer I get is "poor communication." They tell me things like "my boss gives ambiguous directions," "my employees don't listen," and "I can't get people on my team to talk to each other." These comments are not unusual. Most people DO think that communication is the source of most conflicts. But they'd be wrong. In a work context, more conflicts come from structural relationships and personal differences than communication per se.

Organizations create job descriptions, specialized work groups, jurisdictional borders, and authority relationships—all with the intent to facilitate coordination. But in so doing, they separate people and create the potential for conflicts. For instance, departments within organizations have diverse goals. Purchasing is concerned with the timely acquisition of materials and supplies at low prices, marketing's goals concentrate on disposing of finished goods and services and increasing revenues, quality control's attention is focused on improving quality and ensuring that the organization's products meet standards, and production units seek efficiency of operations by maintaining a steady production flow. When groups within an organization seek diverse ends, some of which are inherently at odds, there is increased potential for conflict.

Did you ever meet individuals to whom you took an immediate disliking? Most of the opinions they expressed, you disagreed with. Even insignificant characteristics—the way they cocked their head when they talked or smirked when they smiled—annoyed you. We've all met people like that. And many of us have to work with people like this; people whose values or personality clash with our own. Today's organizations are increasingly diverse in terms of age, gender, race, sexual orientation, and ethnicity. So, not surprisingly, employees differ on the importance they place on general values such as honesty, responsibility, equality, and ambition. They also differ on job-related values such as the importance of family over work or freedom versus authority. These differences often surface in work-related interactions and create significant interpersonal conflicts.

> *The notion that "we can resolve our differences if we just communicate more" is not necessarily true.*

The above is not meant to mean that communication can't be a source of conflict. It can. Differing word connotations, jargon, insufficient exchange of information, poor listening skills, and the like create conflicts. But the notion that "we can resolve our differences if we just communicate more" is not necessarily true. The evidence actually demonstrates that the potential for conflict increases when there is too much communication as well as when there's too little. Apparently, an increase in communication is functional up to a point, whereupon it's possible to overcommunicate. Too much information as well as too little can lay the foundation for conflict.

So when you're trying to manage conflicts, take a thoughtful look at their source. It's more likely that the conflict is coming from work-imposed requirements, dissimilar values, or personality differences than it is from poor communication. And that might influence the actions you take to resolve the conflict.

TRUTH 48

BEWARE OF GROUPTHINK

If you're like me, you've occasionally felt like speaking up in a meeting or group setting but decided against it. Why didn't we speak up? If what we wanted to say didn't fit in with the dominant views of the group, we may have been victims of "groupthink." This is a phenomenon that occurs when group members become so focused on achieving concurrence that the search for consensus overrides any realistic assessment of deviant or unpopular views. It represents a deterioration in an individual's mental efficiency and reality testing as a result of group pressures.

We have all seen the symptoms of the groupthink phenomenon:

1. Group members rationalize any resistance to the assumptions that the group has made. No matter how strongly the evidence may contradict their basic assumptions, members behave so as to reinforce those assumptions continually.

2. Members apply direct pressure on those who momentarily express doubts about any of the group's shared views or

who question the validity of arguments supporting the alternative favored by the majority.

3. Those members who have doubts or hold differing points of view seek to avoid deviating from what appears to be group consensus by keeping silent about misgivings and even minimizing to themselves the importance of their doubts.

4. There appears to be an illusion of unanimity. If someone doesn't speak, it's assumed that he or she sides with the majority view. In other words, abstention becomes viewed as a "Yes" vote.

In studies of historic American foreign policy decisions, groupthink symptoms were found to prevail when government policy-making groups failed—unpreparedness at Pearl Harbor in 1941, the U.S. invasion of North Korea, the Bay of Pigs fiasco, and the escalation of the Vietnam war. More recently, the *Challenger* space shuttle disaster and the failure of the main mirror on the *Hubble* telescope have been linked to decision processes at NASA where groupthink symptoms were evident.

Does groupthink attack all groups? No. It seems to occur most often where there is a clear group identity, where members hold a positive image of their group that they want to protect, and where the group perceives a collective threat to this positive image. So groupthink is not a dissenter-suppression mechanism as much as it's a means for a group to protect its positive image. In the cases of the *Challenger* and *Hubble* fiascos, it was NASA's attempt to confirm its identity as "the elite organization that could do no wrong."

As a manager, what can you do to minimize groupthink? One thing you can do is play an impartial role when you're a group leader. Leaders need to actively seek input from all members and avoid expressing their own opinions, especially in the early stages of deliberation. Another thing is to appoint one group member to play the role of devil's advocate. This member's role is to openly challenge the majority position and offer divergent perspectives. Still another suggestion is to utilize exercises that stimulate active discussion of diverse alternatives without threatening the group and intensifying identity protection. One such exercise is to have group members talk about dangers or risks involved in a decision and delaying discussion of any potential gains. By requiring members to first focus on the negatives of a decision alternative, the group is less likely to stifle dissenting views and more likely to gain an objective evaluation.

> *In groupthink, if someone doesn't speak, it's assumed that he or she sides with the majority view.*

TRUTH 49

How to Reduce Work–Life Conflicts

T he typical employee in the 1960s or 1970s showed up at the workplace Monday through Friday and did his or her job in eight- or nine-hour chunks of time. Both the workplace and hours of work were clearly specified. That's no longer true for many in today's workforce. Employees are increasingly complaining that the line between work and nonwork time has become blurred, creating personal conflicts and stress.

A number of forces have contributed to blurring the lines between employees' work life and personal life. First, the creation of global organizations means their world never sleeps. At any time and on any day, for instance, thousands of DaimlerChrysler employees are working somewhere. The need to consult with colleagues or customers eight or 10 time zones away means that many employees of global firms are "on-call" 24 hours a day. Second, communication technology allows employees to do their work at home, in their car, or on the beach in Tahiti. This lets many people in technical and professional jobs do their work any time and from any place. Third, organizations are asking employees to put in longer hours. For instance, between 1977 and 1997, the average work week increased from 43 to 47 hours, and the number of people working 50 or more hours a week jumped from 24 percent to 37 percent. Finally, fewer families have only a single breadwinner. Today's married employee is typically part of a dual-career couple, often with children at home. In 1980, about half of married women with children worked outside of the home. Today that number is 70 percent. This makes it increasingly difficult for married employees to find the time to fulfill commitments to home, spouse, children, parents, and friends.

Employees are increasingly recognizing that work is squeezing out personal lives and they're not happy about it. For example, recent studies suggest that employees want jobs that give them flexibility in their work schedules so they can better manage work–life conflicts. In addition, the next generation of employees is likely to show similar concerns. A majority of college and university students say that attaining a balance between personal life and work is a primary career goal. They want "a life" as well as a job! Managers who don't help their people achieve work–life balance will find it increasingly hard to attract and retain the most capable and motivated employees.

So, as a manager, what can you do to help your employees who are experiencing work–life conflicts? The overlying answer is: Give employees flexibility and options. The more obvious examples include providing employees with flexible work hours, telecommuting, paid leave time, and on-site support services like child-care and fitness centers. But other options that can make life easier for employees include job sharing, summer day camps for children, elder-care referral services, dry cleaning pick-up and delivery, on-site car maintenance, help in finding jobs for spouses and partners, and free income tax and legal information advisory services.

Many high-tech firms are setting the pace in helping employees balance work–life obligations. For instance, Intel has opened satellite offices around the San Francisco Bay area to accommodate employees who don't want to come into the head office. Cisco Systems has opened a $10 million child-care center that can accommodate up to 440 children. SAS Institute provides top-quality day care to employees' children for only $250 a month. It also has a free on-site medical clinic, and provides 12 holidays a year plus a paid week off

Employees are increasingly recognizing that work is squeezing out personal lives and they're not happy about it.

between Christmas and New Year's. Adobe Systems has introduced telecommuting. And 3Com provides employees with concierge services to handle chores such as dry cleaning, getting movie tickets, and gift shopping.

PART VII

THE TRUTH
ABOUT DESIGNING
JOBS

TRUTH 50

THERE'S NO SUCH THING
AS A "GOOD JOB"

Rob Davidson works as a telephone customer service representative for a photographic supply company. His job consists of taking orders over the phone for company products and handling customer complaints. Rob has been in his job for nearly two years. When he talks about his job, you can see the frustration in his face. He hates his work. He says the job isn't challenging and says management doesn't know what it's doing. It's interesting, however, that Rob's work desk is right next to Jason Stevens. Jason and Rob started their jobs within a month of each other. Both are in their late-30s and married. Where they differ is in their views of their job. In contrast to Rob, Jason is enthusiastic about his work and his employer. "I really love this job. It challenges me. I've got real friendly coworkers. And my boss is very understanding."

Rob and Jason demonstrate that people can look at the same job and evaluate it differently. The reason is that what constitutes a "good job" is not based on some objective or universal standard. Rather, it's in the eye of the beholder. So when you think about hiring employees that will fit well into a job or consider redesigning jobs to increase employee motivation, make sure you assess individual differences. Blanket efforts to make jobs challenging and interesting are likely to fail because they don't take into consideration the individual needs and perceptions of the individuals in those jobs.

Another research-based insight that can help you is that employees' attitudes toward their jobs are strongly influenced by social cues provided by others with whom they interact. Consistent with the previous recognition that there are no objective standards by which people assess the quality of jobs, employees also are susceptible to external influences. Coworkers, supervisors, friends, family members, and customers can shape an employee's attitude toward a job by the things they say and do. For instance, Gary Ling got a summer job working in a British Columbia sawmill. Since jobs were scarce and this one paid particularly well, Gary arrived on his first day of work highly motivated and enthusiastic. Two weeks later, however, this enthusiasm had seriously diminished. What

> *Blanket efforts to make jobs challenging and interesting are likely to fail.*

happened was that his coworkers consistently bad-mouthed their jobs. They said the work was boring, that having to clock in and out proved management didn't trust them, and that supervisors never listened to their opinions. The objective characteristics of Gary's job had not changed in the two-week period; rather, Gary had reconstructed reality based on messages he had received from others. As a manager, you can help positively shape an employee's perceptions by such subtle actions as commenting on the existence or absence of job features such as difficulty, challenge, and autonomy. And you should give as much, or more, attention to employees' perceptions of their jobs as to the actual characteristics of those jobs.

TRUTH 51

NOT EVERYONE WANTS
A CHALLENGING JOB

Does everyone want a challenging job? In spite of all the attention focused by the media, academicians, and social scientists on human potential and the needs of individuals, there is no evidence to support that the vast majority of workers want challenging jobs. Some individuals prefer highly complex and challenging jobs; others prosper in simple, routinized work.

The individual-difference variable that seems to gain the greatest support for explaining who prefers a challenging job and who doesn't is the strength of an individual's needs for personal growth and self-direction at work. Individuals with these higher-order growth needs are more responsive to challenging work. What percentage of rank-and-file workers actually desire higher order need satisfactions and will respond positively to challenging jobs? No current data is available, but a study from the 1970s estimated the figure at about 15 percent. Even after adjusting for changing work attitudes and the growth in white-collar jobs, it seems unlikely that the number today exceeds 40 percent.

The strongest voice advocating challenging jobs has *not* been workers—it's been professors, social science researchers, and media people. Professors, researchers, and journalists undoubtedly made their career choices, to some degree, because they wanted jobs that gave them autonomy, recognition, and challenge. That, of course, is their choice. But for them to project their needs onto the workforce in general is presumptuous.

Not every employee is looking for a challenging job. Many workers meet their higher order needs *off* the job. There are 168 hours in every individual's week. Work rarely consumes more than 30 percent of this time. That leaves considerable opportunity, even for individuals with strong growth needs, to find higher-order need satisfaction outside the workplace. So don't feel you have a responsibility to create challenging jobs for all your employees. For many people, work is something that will never excite or challenge them. And they don't expect to find their growth opportunities at work. Work is merely something they have to do to pay their bills. They can find challenges outside of work on the golf course, fishing, at their local pub, with their friends in social clubs, with their family, and the like.

> *For many people, work is something that will never excite or challenge them.*

TRUTH 52

Four Job-Design Actions That Will Make Employees More Productive

In spite of the reality that there are no ideal job designs, there is substantial evidence that *most* people seem to have four common characteristics they prefer in a job. To the degree that you enrich jobs in your firm by encompassing these characteristics, you increase the probability that people will like their jobs and be motivated to generate high productivity in those jobs.

The following suggestions specify the types of changes in jobs that are most likely to lead to improving their productivity potential.

1. **Combine tasks.** Managers should seek to take existing and fractionalized tasks and put them back together to form a new and larger module of work. This allows employees to do a greater variety of tasks, display more of their talent and skills, and form an identifiable and meaningful whole. It also increases employee "ownership" of the work and improves the likelihood that employees will view their work as meaningful and important. To illustrate, at the Corning Glass Works plant in Medford, Massachusetts, work tasks

were combined to make jobs more interesting. Employees who previously worked on only a single part that went into laboratory hot plates now put entire hot-plate units together.

2. **Establish client relationships.** The client is the user of the product or service that the employee works on (and may be an "internal customer" as well as someone outside the organization). Wherever possible, you should try to establish direct relationships between workers and their clients. This makes the job more interesting and diverse, allows the employee to get direct customer feedback on his or her performance, and gives the employee a greater feeling of ownership over his or her work. Some assembly-line workers at John Deere have been included as part of the sales teams that call on customers. These workers know the products better than any traditional salesperson, and by traveling and speaking with farmers, these hourly workers develop a better understanding of the customers' needs. They also now feel more involved in their jobs because they know what happens to the tractors and machinery they build once it leaves the factory.

3. **Expand jobs vertically.** Vertical expansion gives employees responsibilities and control that were formerly reserved for management. It seeks to partially close the gap between the "doing" and the "controlling" aspects of the job, and it increases employee autonomy. The use of self-managed teams has been effective in increasing verticality. At the L-S Electrogalvanizing Co., in Cleveland, the entire plant is run by self-managed teams, doing many of the tasks that

used to be reserved for management. The teams do their own hiring, scheduling, rotate jobs on their own, establish production targets, set pay scales that are linked to skills, and fire coworkers.

4. *Open feedback channels.* By increasing feedback, employees not only learn how well they are performing their jobs, but also whether their performance is improving, deteriorating, or remaining at a constant level. Ideally, this feedback about performance should be received directly as the

Vertical expansion of jobs gives employees responsibilities and control that were formerly reserved for management.

employee does the job, rather than from management on an occasional basis. Mechanics at General Electric's aircraft engine plant in Durham, North Carolina, get immediate feedback on how they're performing. The plant is designed around self-managed teams, and the team members take on responsibility for providing ongoing feedback to each other so the team can continually improve its performance.

used to be reserved for management. The teams do their own hiring, scheduling, rotate jobs on their own, establish production targets, set pay scales that are linked to skills, and fire coworkers.

4. **Open feedback channels.** By increasing feedback, employees not only learn how well they are performing their jobs, but also whether their performance is improving, deteriorating, or remaining at a constant level. Ideally, this feedback about performance should be received directly as the

Vertical expansion of jobs gives employees responsibilities and control that were formerly reserved for management.

employee does the job, rather than from management on an occasional basis. Mechanics at General Electric's aircraft engine plant in Durham, North Carolina, get immediate feedback on how they're performing. The plant is designed around self-managed teams, and the team members take on responsibility for providing ongoing feedback to each other so the team can continually improve its performance.

PART VIII

THE TRUTH
ABOUT
PERFORMANCE
EVALUATION

TRUTH 53

ANNUAL REVIEWS: THE BEST SURPRISE IS NO SURPRISE!

A number of years ago, Holiday Inn built an advertising campaign around the slogan, "The best surprise is NO surprise!" That slogan would also make good advice today to managers when it comes to giving annual performance reviews.

Few managers enjoy giving performance reviews. Why? There seem to be at least three reasons. First, managers are often uncomfortable discussing performance weaknesses directly with employees. Given that almost every employee could stand to improve in some areas, managers fear a confrontation when presenting negative feedback. This apparently even applies when people give negative feedback to a computer! Bill Gates reports that Microsoft conducted a project that required users to rate their experience with a computer. "When we had the computer the users had worked with ask for an evaluation of its performance, the responses tended to be positive. But when we had a second computer ask the same people to evaluate their encounters with the first machine, the people were significantly more critical. Their reluctance to criticize the first computer 'to its face' suggested that they didn't want to hurt its feelings, even though they knew it was only a machine." Second, many employees tend to become defensive when their weaknesses are pointed out. Instead of accepting the feedback as constructive and a basis for improving performance, some employees challenge the evaluation by criticizing the manager or redirecting blame to someone else. A survey of 151 area managers in Philadelphia, for instance, found that 98 percent of these managers encountered some type of aggression after giving employees negative appraisals. Finally, employees tend to have an inflated assessment of their own performance. Statistically speaking, half of all employees must be below-average performers. But the evidence indicates that the average employee's estimate of his or her own performance level generally falls around the 75th percentile. So even when managers are providing good news, employees are likely to perceive it as not good enough!

Managers are often uncomfortable discussing performance weaknesses directly with employees.

The solution to the performance feedback problem is twofold. First, performance feedback shouldn't be avoided. To the contrary, it needs to be continuous. Don't save up your assessments and then spring them on an employee in his or her annual review. You should be providing feedback all the time. And when the formal review *is* held, the employee shouldn't be confronted with any surprises. The formal annual review should be an aggregate summary of what the employee has been hearing all year long. Second, all managers need to be trained in how to conduct constructive feedback sessions. An effective review—one in which the employee perceives the appraisal as fair, the manager as sincere, and the climate as constructive—can result in the employee leaving the interview in an upbeat mood, informed about the performance areas in which he or she needs to improve, and determined to correct the deficiencies.

TRUTH 54

Don't Blame Me!
The Role of Self-Serving Bias

Did you ever notice that people are pretty good at deflecting blame for failures, yet they're quick to take credit for successes? This is not a random occurrence. In fact, it's predictable.

Our perceptions of people differ from our perceptions of inanimate objects such as desks, machines, or buildings because we make inferences about the actions of people that we don't make about inanimate objects. Nonliving objects are subject to the laws of nature, but they have no beliefs, motives, or intentions. People do. The result is that when we observe people, we attempt to develop explanations of why they behave in certain ways. Our perception and judgment of a person's actions, therefore, will be significantly influenced by the assumptions we make about that person's internal state.

Attribution theory can help us explain the ways in which we judge people differently, depending on what meaning we attribute to a given behavior. Basically, the theory suggests that when we observe an individual's behavior, we attempt to determine whether it was internally or externally caused. That determination, however, depends largely on three factors: (1) distinctiveness, (2) consensus, and (3) consistency. First, let's clarify the differences between internal and external causation and then we'll elaborate on each of the three determining factors.

Internally caused behaviors are those that are believed to be under the personal control of the individual. *Externally* caused behavior is seen as resulting from outside causes; that is, the person is seen as having been forced into the behavior by the situation. If one of your employees is late for work, you might attribute his lateness to his partying into the wee hours of the morning and then oversleeping. This would be an internal attribution. But if you attribute his arriving late to a major automobile accident that tied up traffic on the road that this employee regularly uses, then you would be making an external attribution.

Distinctiveness refers to whether an individual displays different behaviors in different situations. Is the employee who arrives late today also the source of complaints by coworkers for being a "goof-off"? What we want to know is whether this behavior is unusual. If it is, the observer is likely to give the behavior an external attribution. If this action is not unusual, it will probably be judged as internal.

If everyone who is faced with a similar situation responds in the same way, we can say the behavior shows *consensus*. Our late employee's behavior would meet this criterion if all employees who took the same route to work were also late. From an attribution perspective, if consensus is high, you would be expected to give an external attribution to the employee's tardiness, whereas if other employees who took the same route made it to work on time, your conclusion as to causation would be internal.

Finally, an observer looks for *consistency* in a person's actions. Does the person respond the same way over time? Coming in 10 minutes late for work is not perceived in the same way for the employee for whom it is an unusual case (she hasn't been late for several months) as it is for the employee for whom it is part of a routine pattern (she is regularly late two or three times a week). The more consistent the behavior, the more the observer is inclined to attribute it to internal causes.

One of the more interesting findings from attribution theory is that there are errors or biases that distort attributions. For instance, there is a tendency for individuals to attribute their own successes to internal factors such as ability or effort while putting the blame for failure on external factors such

There is a tendency for individuals to attribute their own successes to internal factors such as ability or effort while putting the blame for failure on external factors such as luck.

as luck. This self-serving bias can often make it hard to provide employees with honest and accurate feedback on their performance. Feedback given to employees in performance reviews will be predictably distorted by recipients depending on whether it is positive or negative. So don't be surprised that employees bend over backwards patting themselves on the back for a positive evaluation while looking for external factors to put the blame on when evaluations are negative.

TRUTH 55

THE CASE FOR 360-DEGREE FEEDBACK APPRAISALS: MORE IS BETTER!

Employees at the Cook Children's Health Care System in Fort Worth, Texas, aren't only evaluated by their supervisor. They also get evaluated by patients, coworkers, and people in other departments who interact with them. This is because Cook has implemented 360-degree performance appraisal. It's intended to provide more accurate and diverse input on an employee's performance by seeking feedback from varied sources such as bosses, peers, subordinates, team members, customers, and suppliers. Its popularity is reflected by the fact that nearly 90 percent of Fortune 1000 firms now use this approach for their employee appraisals.

The 360-degree feedback system recognizes that performance varies across contexts and that individuals behave differently with different constituencies. By getting feedback from various constituencies, the reliability of the performance evaluation is increased. So, 360-degree appraisals capture the reality that an employee's performance typically is made up of multiple behaviors and that access to observing those different behaviors varies among constituencies. Multiple evaluations by different constituencies have been found to capture this variety of behavior and improve the quality of the performance appraisal data.

In the typical 360-degree appraisal system, employees are evaluated by eight to 12 people. Ideally, they should be individuals who work closely with the employee and have direct contact in assessing his or her performance. It's been found that 360-degree feedback works best with employees who work in teams or at a distance from their bosses. In the former case, team members are better able to accurately assess an employee's contribution than his or her immediate supervisor. In the latter case, remote bosses often have little day-to-day contact with the em-

Nearly 90 percent of Fortune 1000 firms now use 360-degree feedback for their employee appraisals.

ployee, and evaluations tend to be inaccurate because they're based on limited and selected bits of information. In the case of a sales rep who is on the road most of the time, the customers he or she meets with regularly can offer performance insights that a supervisor would never be privy to.

Jay Marshall found 360-degree feedback helpful when he was a partner at Booz Allen. In charge of a team of about 75 consultants, Marshall learned through a 360-degree review that he had "become invisible" to the consultants he was overseeing. The feedback he got made him realize that he was spending too much time trying to keep the client happy and shortchanging his team of the time they needed from him. That feedback wouldn't have been possible from his boss or other superiors who never visited his job site.

The major problem you need to be aware of with these appraisals is the tendency of evaluators to use them as a means of "getting even" with an employee. This can be particularly troublesome with input provided by subordinates and peers. Since reviews are usually anonymous, evaluators with an axe to grind can use the system to even scores. To help alleviate this problem, most companies allow employees to choose which subordinates and peers they want to review them. While this can create a tendency for individuals to selectively "choose friends," this bias can be reduced by ensuring that a substantial number of evaluations are sought. A sample of only three or four evaluations can be easily manipulated. But a sample of 10 or 12 is likely to provide a reasonably accurate picture of the evaluatee's strengths and weaknesses.

PART IX

THE TRUTH
ABOUT COPING
WITH CHANGE

TRUTH 56

MOST PEOPLE RESIST ANY CHANGE THAT DOESN'T JINGLE IN THEIR POCKETS!

One of the most well-documented findings from studies of individual and organizational behavior is that organizations and their members resist change. In one sense, this is positive. It provides a degree of stability and predictability to behavior. If there weren't some resistance, organizational behavior would take on characteristics of chaotic randomness. Resistance to change can also be a source of functional conflict. For example, resistance to a reorganization plan or a change in a product line can stimulate a healthy debate over the merits of the idea and result in a better decision. But there is a definite downside to resistance to change. It hinders adaptation and progress.

Resistance to change doesn't necessarily surface in standardized ways. Resistance can be overt, implicit, immediate, or deferred. It's easiest for management to deal with resistance when it is overt and immediate. For instance, a change is proposed and employees quickly respond by voicing complaints, engaging in a work slowdown, threatening to go on strike, or the like. The greater challenge is managing resistance that is implicit or deferred. Implicit resistance efforts are more subtle—loss of loyalty to the organization, loss of motivation to work, increased errors or mistakes, increased absenteeism due to "sickness"—and hence more difficult to recognize. Similarly, deferred actions cloud the link between the source of the resistance and the reaction to it. A change may produce what appears to be only a minimal reaction at the time it is initiated, but then resistance surfaces weeks, months, or even years later. Or a single change that in and of itself might have little impact becomes the straw that breaks the camel's back. Reactions to change can build up and then explode in some response that seems totally out of proportion to the change action it follows. The resistance, of course, has merely been deferred and stockpiled. What surfaces is a response to an accumulation of previous changes.

Resistance to change can come from either the individual or the organization. Let me start by highlighting some individual sources of resistance to change: habit, security, economic factors, and fear of the unknown.

We're all creatures of *habit*. Life is complex enough; we don't need to consider the full range of options for the hundreds of decisions we have to make every day. To cope with this complexity, we all rely on habits or programmed responses. But when confronted with change, this tendency to respond in our accustomed ways becomes a source of resistance. People with a high need for *security* are likely to resist change because it threatens their feelings of safety. Another source of individual resistance is concern that changes will lower one's income. Changes in job tasks or established work routines also can arouse *economic fears* if people are concerned that they won't be able to perform the new tasks or routines to their previous standards, especially when pay is closely tied to productivity.

Changes substitute ambiguity and uncertainty for the known. You trade the known for the *unknown* and the fear or insecurity that goes with it.

Organizations, by their very nature, are conservative. They actively resist change through structural and group inertia, and threats to member expertise, power relationships, and established resource allocations.

Organizations have built-in mechanisms to produce stability. For example, the selection process systematically selects certain people in and certain people out. Training and other socialization techniques reinforce specific role requirements and skills. Formalization provides job descriptions, rules, and procedures for employees to follow. So the people who are hired into an organization are chosen for fit; they are then shaped and directed to behave in certain ways. When an organization is confronted with change, this *structural inertia* acts as a counterbalance to sustain

Resistance to change hinders adaptation and progress.

stability. And even if individuals want to change their behavior, group norms may act as a constraint. Changes in organizational patterns may threaten the expertise of specialized groups. Any redistribution of decision-making authority can threaten long-established power relationships within the organization. Those groups in the organization that control sizable resources often see change as a threat. They tend to be content with the way things are. Those that most benefit from the current allocation of resources often feel threatened by changes that may affect future allocations.

What does all this mean to you as a manager? First, initiating change is an important part of most managers' job. Second, expect resistance to change to come in a number of forms. And finally, be prepared to undermine this resistance. How? By actions such as providing rewards for accepting change, communicating reasons for why a change is necessary, and including people who will be affected by the change to participate in change decisions.

TRUTH 57

You CAN Teach
an Old Dog New Tricks

W estern cultures have historically been biased toward youth. The problem is so serious that we have enacted legislation that specifically prohibits age discrimination in the workplace. But many of us still carry around a prejudice against hiring or investing in employees over age 50. Part of this prejudice, undoubtedly, reflects the widely-held stereotype that older workers have difficulties in adapting to new methods and techniques. Studies consistently demonstrate that older employees are *perceived* as being relatively inflexible, resistant to change, and less trainable than their younger counterparts, particularly with respect to information technology skills. But these perceptions are wrong.

The evidence indicates that older workers want to learn and are just as capable of learning as any other employee group. Older workers do seem to be somewhat less efficient in acquiring complex or demanding skills. That is, they may take longer to train. But once trained, they perform at comparable levels to younger workers.

The ability to acquire the skills, knowledge, or behavior necessary to perform a job at a given level—that is, trainability—has been the subject of much research. And the evidence indicates that there are differences between people in their trainability. A number of individual difference factors (such as ability, motivational level, and personality) have been found to significantly influence learning and training outcomes. Age, however, has not been found to influence these outcomes.

Just because older workers are trainable, of course, is not justification for hiring them. We want to make sure that they're competitive in terms of job performance. How do they stack up on factors like job commitment, absenteeism, productivity, and satisfaction? The evidence might surprise you. Older workers are more committed in that they're less likely to quit their jobs than their younger counterparts. Older employees also have lower rates of avoidable absence. And age and job performance have been found to be unrelated, so age doesn't seem to be a hindrance.

Older workers want to learn and are just as capable of learning as any other employee group.

Only in jobs with extremely demanding heavy manual labor requirements do we find declines in productivity due to age. Finally, workers 65 and over record higher job satisfaction scores than their coworkers aged 45–64.

The above evidence is good news for managers. We're entering a period where there will be a draining labor pool. Generation X has only 66 million members, and it's trying to replace the larger Baby Boomer generation, which has 76 million. A large part of this deficit can be filled with older workers. They have the skills and many of them have the desire or need to continue working past traditional retirement ages of 62 or 65. Tapping into the older-worker labor supply should provide organizations with a pool of skilled, motivated, and committed applicants.

TRUTH 58

USE PARTICIPATION TO
REDUCE RESISTANCE TO CHANGE

Having employees participate in decisions that affect them is no panacea. Participation has only a modest influence on factors such as employee productivity, motivation, and job satisfaction. But it's a potent force for combating resistance to change.

It's difficult for individuals to resist a change decision in which they participated. So prior to making a change, consider whether the conditions are right for using participation. What are those conditions? There must be adequate time to participate, the issues in which the employees are asked to get involved in must be relevant to their interests, the employees must have the ability (including intelligence, technical knowledge, and communication skills) to participate, and the organization's culture must support employee involvement. On this last point, employees aren't likely to take participation efforts seriously when the company's culture has long been dominated by autocratic decision making and ignoring employee input.

When those conditions exist, participation can reduce resistance, obtain commitment, and increase the quality of the change decision. And companies have found varied ways of bringing employees into decisions that involve change. Suggestion programs, for instance, identify and reward employees who offer ideas for change. Quality circles provide opportunities for groups of employees, in shared areas of responsibility, to discuss their quality problems, investigate causes of those problems, and recommend solutions to management. Many firms are adding employee representatives to executive task forces designed to address major changes. And an increasing number of North American companies are adopting the popular Western European approach of including employee representatives on their board of directors.

It's difficult for individuals to resist a change decision in which they participated.

TRUTH 59

LAYOFFS ARE AS TOUGH ON SURVIVORS AS THOSE WHO GET LAID OFF

In the spring and summer of 2001, you couldn't pick up a business periodical without reading about another major company laying off employees. Companies as varied as Lucent Technologies, Sara Lee, Intel, Walt Disney, General Electric, J.C. Penney, and 3M all announced massive layoffs. When these announcements are made, attention naturally flows to those individuals who've lost their jobs. We expect that they're likely to suffer from depression, anxiety, and similar negative feelings. And companies respond by offering layoff victims outplacement services, psychological counseling, support groups, and extended benefit programs. While we certainly don't want to downplay the trauma that layoffs can have on those who have lost their jobs, managers often ignore the impact that downsizing has on the survivors. There is an increasing amount of evidence that indicates that layoffs have severe effects on those employees who remain after layoffs. And managers who ignore these effects and fail to address them are likely to suffer serious drops in their organization's performance.

The evidence shows both victims and survivors experience similar feelings of frustration, anxiety, and loss. But layoff victims get to move on and start over with a clean slate. This isn't true of survivors. They're likely to suffer from layoff survivor sickness. Symptoms of this sickness include job insecurity, perceptions of unfairness, depression, stress from increased workloads, fear of change, loss of loyalty and commitment, reduced risk taking and motivation, unwillingness to do anything beyond the required minimum, feelings of not being kept well informed, and a loss of confidence in upper management.

Managers often ignore the impact that downsizing has on the survivors.

What can managers do to deal with layoff survivor sickness? A four-step approach has been suggested:

Step 1: **Get the process right.** Well-designed layoff processes won't cure survivor sickness, but they keep survivors from sinking into deeper survivor symptoms. Characteristics of a well-designed process include: Make the cuts clear and quick. Provide abundant information to both victims and survivors. Give layoff victims adequate prior notification. Be emotionally honest and authentic in all communications. Explain decisions openly and in terms of fairness. And, if possible, allow employees to participate.

Step 2: **Let people grieve to deal with repressed feelings and emotions.** Even in the best-handled layoffs, survivors feel violated. They must release their feelings before they can go on. They need to go through the same grieving process that one goes through after a death in the family. Use of groups is one of the most effective and efficient means of bringing survivor emotions to the surface. In a relatively short time, most natural work teams can make a great deal of progress in unblocking and addressing their survivor feelings.

Step 3: *Break the chain of organizational dependence.* This step tries to help survivors recapture their sense of control and self-esteem. While Steps 1 and 2 react to existing layoff survivor symptoms, this step offers the possibility of preventing the sickness in the first place by moving people from organizational dependency to self-directed careers. Today's workplace requires employees to build transferable skills and have independence from their employers. An employee's loyalty is no longer to the organization but to his or her own career. The breaking of this dependency relationship is essentially an individual effort.

Step 4: *Reshape the organization's systems to lessen processes that create dependency.* This final step seeks to help people immunize themselves against survivor sickness. Organizations historically did a lot to create co-dependency: Seniority systems for promotions and rewards; loyalty expectations; promotion from within; long-term socialization processes to shape people into "desired employees"; long-term career planning; and non-transferable corporate pension plans. Organizations have to detach themselves from these paternalistic practices.

PART X

SOME FINAL THOUGHTS ABOUT MANAGING BEHAVIOR

TRUTH 60

I'll See It When I Believe It

Most of us recognize the link between attitudes and behavior. Advertisers, for instance, invest a lot of money trying to get us to feel good about their product. The reason is that they realize that attitudes influence behavior. You're more likely to buy a Nike product if you have a positive view of the Nike company and its product line. If its basketball shoes are good enough for Michael Jordan, it sure ought to be good enough for me!

In a similar focus on attitudes and behavior, managers typically are concerned with employee satisfaction because they think it's linked to productivity. A happy worker is more likely to be a productive worker. But there is an interesting stream of evidence that indicates that behavior influences attitudes as much as the reverse. Specifically, we find that attitudes are often used after the fact to make sense out of an action that has already occurred. We call this self-perception theory.

When asked about an attitude toward some object, individuals recall their behavior relevant to that object and then infer their attitude from their past behavior. So if an employee were asked about her feelings about being a training specialist at Motorola, she would likely think, "I've had this same job at Motorola as a trainer for 10 years. Nobody forced me to stay on this job. So I must like it!" Self-perception theory, therefore, argues that attitudes are used, after the fact, to make sense out of an action that has already occurred rather than as devices that precede and guide action. Attitudes are just casual verbal statements. When people are asked about their attitudes, and they don't have strong convictions or feelings, self-perception theory says they tend to create plausible answers.

Attitudes are often used after the fact to make sense out of an action that has already occurred.

Self-perception theory has been well supported. While the traditional *attitude causes behavior* relationship is generally positive, the *behavior causes attitude* relationship is stronger. This is particularly true when attitudes are vague and ambiguous. When employees have had few experiences regarding an attitude issue or have given little previous thought to it, they'll tend to infer their attitudes from their behavior. However, when their attitudes have been established for a while and are well defined, those attitudes are likely to guide their behavior.

What does this mean for managing people at work? It has implications for such varied activities as conducting attitude surveys and managing change. Attitude surveys, for instance, are a frequently used tool to tap attitudes toward work, including job satisfaction. But is the effort to improve attitudes a worthwhile effort if changes don't come easy or if they don't lead to improvements in employee behavior? Maybe the place to begin is with the employee's behavior itself. Focus specifically on those direct factors that can help an employee be more productive. When employees are more productive, they feel better about themselves. They also are more likely to reap rewards—wage increases, promotions, praise from their supervisor, and respect from coworkers. This, in turn, is likely to make employees feel better about their job and employer.

TRUTH 61

FIRST IMPRESSIONS DO COUNT!

When we meet someone for the first time, we notice a number of things about that person—physical characteristics, clothes, firmness of handshake, gestures, tone of voice, and the like. We then use these impressions to fit the person into ready-made categories. And this early categorization, formed quickly and on the basis of minimal information, tends to hold greater weight than impressions and information received later.

Psychologists refer to the power of first impressions as the primacy effect. Essentially, it just means that first impressions influence latter impressions. What's important from our perspective is that the primacy effect carries a lot of weight when we assess other people and, maybe more importantly, that first impressions of people are not very accurate.

Why do we rely so heavily on first impressions? Basically, we're looking for a shortcut. When we meet new people, we want to categorize them so that we can process and understand information about them quickly. The error is compounded by the fact that we tend to cling to our first impressions. When later information is received that might contradict that first impression, we tend to discount, misrepresent, reinterpret, or even ignore it.

The best evidence on first impressions comes from research on employment interviews. Findings clearly demonstrate that first impressions count. More specifically, the information processed first has a greater effect on later judgments than subsequent information does.

Research on applicant appearance confirms the power of first impressions. Studies have looked at assessments made of applicants before the actual interview—that brief period in which the applicant walks into an interview room, exchanges greetings with the interviewer, sits down, and engages in minor chit-chat. The evidence indicates that the way applicants walk, talk, dress, and look can have a great impact on the interviewer's evaluation of applicant qualifications. Facial attractiveness seems to be particularly influential. Applicants who are highly attractive are evaluated as more qualified for a variety of jobs than those who are unattractive.

> *When later information is received that might contradict our first impression, we tend to discount, misrepresent, reinterpret, or even ignore it.*

Initial positive impressions even reshape the interview itself. Positive first impressions lead interviewers to speak in a more pleasant interpersonal style and to ask less-threatening questions.

A final body of confirmative research finds that interviewers' post-interview evaluations of applicants conform, to a substantial degree, to their pre-interview impressions. That is, those first impressions carry considerable weight in shaping the interviewers' final evaluations, regardless of what actually transpired in the interview itself. This latter conclusion assumes that the interview elicits no highly negative information.

Based on numerous studies of the interview process, we can say that first impressions are powerful influences on outcomes. Instead of using the interviews to gather unbiased information, interviewers typically use the process to merely confirm first impressions.

Can managers do anything to lessen the power of first impressions? First, we suggest that you avoid the tendency to make quick initial judgements. Try to stay neutral when you meet someone for the first time. The more time that goes by before you make a conclusion, the better you'll know the person and the more accurate your assessment. Second, keep your mind open for new information that may contradict earlier assessments. Think of any early impression as a working hypothesis that you're constantly testing for its accuracy.

TRUTH 62

PEOPLE AREN'T COMPLETELY RATIONAL: DON'T IGNORE EMOTIONS!

Emotions are part of our lives. That is, we not only think, we feel! But the field of management has been guilty for a long time of treating employees as if they're nonemotional. All work behavior is assumed to be fully rational. While this makes for simpler analysis of workplace behavior, it also creates highly unrealistic and inaccurate assessments.

Why have management studies tended to downplay emotions? We can offer two possible explanations. The first is the *myth of rationality*. Since the late 19th century and the rise of scientific management, organizations have been specifically designed with the objective of trying to control emotions. A well-run organization was viewed as one that successfully eliminated frustration, fear, anger, love, hate, joy, grief, and similar feelings. Such emotions were the antithesis of rationality. So while managers knew that emotions were an inseparable part of everyday life, they tried to create organizations that were emotion-free. That, of course, was not possible. The second factor was the belief that *emotions of any kind were disruptive*. When emotions were considered, the discussion focused on strong negative emotions—especially anger—that interferred with an employee's ability to do his or her job effectively. Emotions were rarely viewed as being constructive or able to stimulate performance-enhancing behaviors.

Certainly some emotions, particularly when exhibited at the wrong time, can reduce employee performance. But this doesn't change the reality that employees bring an emotional component with them to work every day and that no discussion of organizational behavior could be comprehensive or accurate without considering the role of emotions in workplace behavior.

How do you read someone's emotions? The easiest way to find out what someone is feeling is to ask them. But relying on verbal responses has two drawbacks. First, almost all of us conceal our emotions to some extent for privacy and to reflect social expectations. Second, even if we want to verbally convey our feelings, we may be unable to express them. So you should also look for nonverbal cues like facial expressions, gestures, body movements, and physical distance that can provide additional insights into what a person is feeling. Something as subtle as the distance someone chooses to position himself or herself from you can convey their feelings, or lack thereof, of intimacy, aggressiveness, repugnance, or withdrawal. Finally, don't ignore communication that goes beyond the specific spoken words. Look for how people say things through their pitch, amplitude, and rate of speech.

Let me conclude by briefly mentioning just three areas where an understanding of emotions can help managers be more effective—employee selection, motivation, and managing interpersonal conflicts.

Studies of emotional intelligence (EI)—the ability to cope with situational demands and pressures—have found that people with high EI scores are better at relating to others. In hiring, especially in jobs that demand a high degree of social interaction, you should look for people with high emotional intelligence.

> *In hiring, especially in jobs that demand a high degree of social interaction, you should look for people with high emotional intelligence.*

Most motivation theories propose that individuals engage in rational exchange: trading effort for pay, security, promotions, and similar rewards. But people aren't cold, unfeeling machines. Their perceptions and calculations of situations are filled with emotional content that significantly influences how much effort they exert. For instance, people who are highly motivated in their jobs are emotionally committed. If you want employees who are motivated and will sustain their effort, you need to get them emotionally immersed in their work as well as physically and cognitively.

Finally, few issues are more intertwined with emotions than interpersonal conflicts at work. Whenever conflicts arise, you can be fairly certain that emotions are also surfacing. The manager who ignores the emotional elements in conflicts, focusing singularly on rational and task concerns, is unlikely to be very effective in resolving those conflicts.

TRUTH 63

BEWARE OF THE QUICK FIX

Too many modern managers are like compulsive dieters. They try the latest craze for a few days (or months), and then move restlessly on to the next craze. The sad news for managers is the same that we'd offer dieters: There is no quick fix!

That said, there is no shortage of consultants, management-development professionals, and business journalists ready to pitch instant solutions to complex management problems. They've been doing it for more than four decades. In the 1960s, the list of "instant panaceas" included MBO; Planning, Programming, and Budgeting Systems (PPBS); Theory Y management; sensitivity training; job enrichment; PERT; and the BCG Matrix. In the 1970s, you had centralized strategic planning, matrix organization designs, management by committee, flextime, and zero-base budgeting. The 1980s gave us intrapreneurship, quality circles, Theory Z, just-in-time inventory systems, Deming's 14 principles, self-managed teams, and skunk works. And the 1990s offered up strategic alliances, exploiting core competencies, pay for performance, TQM, reengineering, mass customization, charismatic leadership, visionary leadership, emotional intelligence, boundaryless organizations, learning organizations, outsourcing, and empowerment. While the new century is only a couple of years old, we've already been told about the virtues of work–family balance, e-leadership, virtual organizations, knowledge management, and workplace spirituality.

Managers, like all people, are susceptible to fads. My message here is merely to warn managers: Buyer beware! There will always be someone selling the latest management technique. And unfortunately, rather than being presented in a contingency framework, with recognition that they work best under certain circumstances and are likely to be ineffective in other circumstances, advocates have tended to offer them as instant solutions. At the extreme, it can drive managers to run from one quick fix to another. This was driven home when a frustrated executive recently told me, "In the past couple of years, we've heard that profit is more important than revenue, that quality is more important than profit, that our people are more important than quality, that customers are more important than our people, that big customers are more important than small customers, and that growth is the key to our success."

> *No single new idea can make a mediocre manager excellent or lead to turning around a poorly managed company.*

The common theme among these "quick fixes," like diet books, is that they're sold as universal solutions to complex problems. They're rarely presented in a situational or contingency perspective. And that's the mistake. Each, in its own way, has something to offer managers. These techniques are tools in a tool chest. But just as a carpenter can't solve every problem with a hammer, managers can't solve every problem with self-managed teams or TQM. There are no shortcuts to the complex job of managing. You need to treat new ideas and concepts as tools that can help you be more effective in your job. But no single new idea can make a mediocre manager excellent or lead to turning around a poorly managed company.

REFERENCES

1. Based on A. Davis-Blake and J. Pfeffer, "Just a Mirage: The Search for Dispositional Effects in Organizational Research," *Academy of Management Review*, July 1989, pp. 385–400.

2. Based on J.A. Breaugh, "Realistic Job Previews: A Critical Appraisal and Future Research Directions," *Academy of Management Review*, October 1983, pp. 612–19; J.M. Phillips, "Effects of Realistic Job Previews on Multiple Organizational Outcomes: A Meta-Analysis," *Academy of Management Journal*, December 1998, pp. 673–90; and C. Hymowitz, "Immigrant Couple Use Their Survival Skills to Build Tech Success," *Wall Street Journal*, February 12, 2001, p. B1.

3. Based on W.C. Donaghy, *The Interview: Skills and Applications* (Glenview, Ill: Scott Foresman, 1984), pp. 245–80; and J.M. Jenks and B.L.P. Zevnik, "ABCs of Job Interviewing," *Harvard Business Review*, July–August 1989, pp. 38–42.

4. Based on R.D. Arvey, B.P. McCall, T.J. Bouchard, Jr., and P. Taubman, "Genetic Influences on Job Satisfaction and Work Values," *Personality and Individual Differences*, July 1994, pp. 21–33; D. Lykken and A. Tellegen, "Happiness Is a Stochastic Phenomenon," *Psychological Science*, May 1996, pp. 186–89; and T.A. Judge, E.A. Locke, C.C. Durham, and A.N. Kluger, "Dispositional Effects on Job and Life Satisfaction: The Role of Core Evaluations," *Journal of Applied Psychology*, February 1998, pp. 17–34.

5. Based on D.W. Organ, *Organizational Citizenship Behavior: The Good Soldier Syndrome* (Lexington, MA: Lexington Books, 1988); M.A. Konovsky and D.W. Organ, "Dispositional and Contextual Determinants of Organizational Citizenship Behavior," *Journal of Organizational Behavior*, May 1996, pp. 253–66; and P.M. Podsakoff, S.B. MacKenzie, J.B. Paine, and D.G. Bachrach, "Organizational Citizenship Behaviors: A Critical Review of the Theoretical and Empirical Literature and Suggestions for Future Research," *Journal of Management*, vol. 26, no. 3, 2000, pp. 543–48.

6. Based on R.J. Hernstein and C. Murray, *The Bell Curve: Intelligence and Class Structure in American Life* (New York: Free Press, 1994); M.J. Ree, J.A. Earles, and M.S. Teachout, "Predicting Job Performance: Not Much More Than g," *Journal of Applied Psychology*, August 1994, pp. 518–24; "Mainstream Science on Intelligence," *Wall Street Journal*, December 13, 1994, p. A18; and W. Wright, *Born That Way: Genes, Behavior, Personality* (New York: Knopf, 1998).

7. Based on R.R. Reilly and G.T. Chao, "Validity and Fairness of Some Alternative Employee Selection Procedures," *Personnel Psychology*, Spring 1982, pp. 1–62; and M. Brown, "Reference Checking: The Law is on Your Side," *Human Resource Measurements*, December 1991, pp. 4–5.

8. Based on J.M. Digman, "Personality Structure: Emergence of the Five-Factor Model," in M.R. Rosenzweig and L.W. Porter (eds.), *Annual Review of Psychology*, vol. 41 (Palo Alto, CA: Annual Reviews, 1990), pp. 417–40; P.H. Raymark, M.J. Schmit, and R.M. Guion, "Identifying Potentially Useful Personality Constructs for Employee Selection," *Personnel Psychology*, Autumn 1997, pp. 723–36; A.J. Vinchur, J.S. Schippmann, F.S. Switzer III, and P.L. Roth, "A Meta-Analytic Review of Predictors of Job Performance for Salespeople," *Journal of Applied Psychology*, August 1998, pp. 586–97; G.M. Hurtz and J.J. Donovan, "Personality and Job Performance: The Big Five Revisited," *Journal of Applied Psychology*,

December 2000, pp. 869–79; and T.A. Judge and J.E. Bono, "Relationship of Core Self-Evaluations Traits—Self Esteem, Generalized Self-Efficacy, Locus of Control, and Emotional Stability—With Job Satisfaction and Job Performance: A Meta-Analysis," *Journal of Applied Psychology*, February 2001, pp. 80–92.

9. Based on C.A. O'Reilly III, J. Chatman, and D.F. Caldwell, "People and Organizational Culture: A Profile Comparison Approach to Assessing Person-Organization Fit," *Academy of Management Journal*, September 1991, pp. 487–516; B. Schneider, H.W. Goldstein, and D.B. Smith, "The ASA Framework: An Update," *Personnel Psychology*, Winter 1995, pp. 747–73; A.L. Kristof, "Person-Organization Fit: An Integrative Review of Its Conceptualizations, Measurement, and Implications," *Personnel Psychology*, Spring 1996, pp. 1–49; and B. Schneider, D.B. Smith, S. Taylor, and J. Fleenor, "Personality and Organizations: A Test of the Homogeneity of Personality Hypothesis," *Journal of Applied Psychology*, June 1998, pp. 462–70.

10. Based on J.L. Holland, *Making Vocational Choices: A Theory of Vocational Personalities and Work Environments* (Odessa, FL: Psychological Assessment Resources, 1997); J.L. Holland and G.D. Gottfredson, "Studies of the Hexagonal Model: An Evaluation (or, The Perils of Stalking the Perfect Hexagon)," *Journal of Vocational Behavior*, April 1992, pp. 158–70; T.J. Tracey and J. Rounds, "Evaluating Holland's and Gati's Vocational-Interest Models: A Structural Meta-Analysis," *Psychological Bulletin*, March 1993, pp. 229–46; and F. De Fruyt and I. Mervielde, "RIASEC Types and Big Five Traits as Predictors of Employment Status and Nature of Employment," *Personnel Psychology*, Autumn 1999, pp. 701–27.

11. Based on J. Van Maanen, "People Processing: Strategies of Organizational Socialization," *Organizational Dynamics*, Summer 1978, pp. 19–36; and E.H. Schein, "Organizational Culture," *American Psychologist*, February 1990, p. 116.

12   Based on V.H. Vroom, *Work and Motivation* (New York: John Wiley, 1964); L. Reinharth and M.A. Wahba, "Expectancy Theory as a Predictor of Work Motivation, Effort Expenditure, and Job Performance," *Academy of Management Journal*, September 1975, pp. 502–37; and W. Van Eerde and H. Thierry, "Vroom's Expectancy Models and Work-Related Criteria: A Meta-Analysis," *Journal of Applied Psychology*, October 1996, pp. 575–86.

13.   Based on M.T. Iaffaldano and P.M. Muchinsky, "Job Satisfaction and Job Performance: A Meta-Analysis," *Psychological Bulletin*, March 1985, pp. 251–73; M.M. Petty, G.W. McGee, and J.W. Cavender, "A Meta-Analysis of the Relationship Between Individual Job Satisfaction and Individual Performance," *Academy of Management Review*, October 1984, pp. 712–21; and R.A. Katzell, D.E. Thompson, and R.A. Guzzo, "How Job Satisfaction and Job Performance Are and Are Not Linked," in C.J. Cranny, P.C. Smith, and E.F. Stone (eds.), *Job Satisfaction* (New York: Lexington Books, 1992), pp. 195–217.

14   Based on A. Wellner, "Get Ready for Generation Next," *Training*, February 1999, pp. 42–48; R. Zemke, C. Raines, and B. Filipczak, *Generations at Work: Managing the Clash of Veterans, Boomers, Xers, and Nexters in Your Workplace* (New York: AMACOM, 1999); C. Penttila, "Generational Gyrations," *Entrepreneur*, April 2001, pp. 102–05; and R. Zemke, "Here Come the Millennials," *Training*, July 2001, pp. 44–49.

15.   Based on E.A. Locke and G.P. Latham, *A Theory of Goal Setting and Task Performance* (Upper Saddle River, NJ: Prentice Hall, 1990); J.C. Wofford, V.L. Goodwin, and S. Premack, "Meta-Analysis of the Antecedents of Personal Goal Level and of the Antecedents and Consequences of Goal Commitment," *Journal of Management*, vol. 18, no. 3, 1992, pp. 595–615; and E.A. Locke, "Motivation Through Conscious Goal Setting," *Applied and Preventive Psychology*, vol. 5, 1996, pp. 117–24.

16. Based on M. Erez, P.C. Earley, and C.L. Hulin, "The Impact of Participation on Goal Acceptance and Performance: A Two-Step Model," *Academy of Management Journal*, March 1985, pp. 50–66; J.A. Wagner III, "Participation's Effects on Performance and Satisfaction: A Reconsideration of Research Evidence," *Academy of Management Review*, April 1994, pp. 312–30; and D. Collins, "The Ethical Superiority and Inevitability of Participatory Management as an Organizational System," *Organization Science*, September–October 1997, pp. 489–507.

17. Based on the work of M. Csikszentmihalyi. See *Flow: The Psychology of Optimal Experience* (New York: HarperCollins, 1990); and *Finding Flow* (New York: Basic Books, 1997).

18. Based on J. Thaler, "The Web at Work," *Seattle Times*, April 4, 1999, p. C1; E. deLisser, "One-Click Commerce: What People Do Now to Goof Off at Work," *Wall Street Journal*, September 24, 1999, p. A1; M. Conlin, "Workers, Surf at Your Own Risk," *Business Week*, June 12, 2000, p. 105; P. Sloan, "New Ways to Goof Off at Work," *U.S. News & World Report*, September 4, 2000, pp. 42–43; A. Cohen, "No Web For You!" *Fortune*, October 30, 2000, pp. F208[B]–[L]; "Canadian Workers Waste 800 Million Hours On the Web," *Manpower Argus*, January 2001, p. 8; "Electronic Surveillance of Employees Is On the Rise in the U.S.," *Manpower Argus*, January 2001, p. 8; and V.K.G. Lim, G.L. Loo, and T.S.H. Teo, "Perceived Injustice, Neutralization, and Cyberloafing at the Workplace," paper presented at the Academy of Management Conference, Washington, DC, August 2001.

19. Based on T. Alessandra and P. Hunsaker, *Communicating at Work* (New York: Simon & Shuster, 1993), pp. 86–90.

20. Based on "The Cop-Out Cops," *National Observer*, August 3, 1974; and S. Kerr, "On the Folly of Rewarding A, While Hoping for B," *Academy of Management Executive*, February 1995, pp. 7–14.

21. Based on J.S. Adams, "Inequity in Social Exchanges," in L. Berkowitz (ed.), *Advances in Experimental Social Psychology* (New York: Academic Press, 1965), pp. 267–300; and R.T. Mowday, "Equity Theory Predictions of Behavior in Organizations," in R. Steers, L.W. Porter, and G. Bigley (eds.), *Motivation and Work Behavior*, 6th ed. (New York: McGraw-Hill, 1996), pp. 111–31.

22. Based on S. Caudron, "The Top 20 Ways to Motivate Employees," *Industry Week*, April 3, 1995, p. 14; B. Nelson, "Try Praise," *INC.*, September 1996, p. 115; R. Maynard, "How to Motivate Low-Wage Workers," *Nation's Business*, May 1997, pp. 35–39; and B. Leonard, "The Key to Unlocking an Inexpensive Recognition Plan," *HR Magazine*, October 1999, p. 26.

23. Based on D. Hage and J. Impoco, "Jawboning the Jobs," *U.S. News & World Report*, August 9, 1993, p. 53; M.P. Cronin, "One Life to Live," *INC.*, July 1993, pp. 56–60; and S.C. Lundin, H. Paul, and J. Christensen, *Fish!* (New York: Hyperion, 2000).

24. Based on M. Blumberg and C.D. Pringle, "The Missing Opportunity in Organizational Research: Some Implications for a Theory of Work Performance," *Academy of Management Review*, October 1982, pp. 560–69; and J. Hall, "Americans Know How to Be Productive If Managers Will Let Them," *Organizational Dynamics*, Winter 1994, pp. 33–46.

25. Based on F. Bartolome, "Nobody Trusts the Boss Completely—Now What?," *Harvard Business Review*, March–April 1989, pp. 135–42; J.K. Butler, Jr., "Toward Understanding the Measuring Conditions of Trust: Evolution of a Condition of Trust Inventory," *Journal of Management*, September 1991, pp. 643–63; P.L. Schindler and C.C. Thomas, "The Structure of Interpersonal Trust in the Workplace," *Psychological Reports*, October 1993, pp. 563–73; D.J. McAllister, "Affect- and Cognition-Based Trust as Foundations for Interpersonal Cooperation in Organizations," *Academy of Management Journal*, February 1995, p. 25; "Chrysler: Not Quite So Equal," *Business*

Week, November 13, 2000, p. 14; R. Pillai, C.A. Schriesheim, and E.S. Williams, "Fairness Perceptions and Trust as Mediators for Transformational and Transactional Leadership: A Two-Sample Study," *Journal of Management*, vol. 25, no. 6, 1999, pp. 897–933; J. Cunningham and J. MacGregor, "Trust and the Design of Work: Complementary Constructs in Satisfaction and Performance," *Human Relations*, December 2000, pp. 1575–91; K.T. Dirks and D.L. Ferrin, "The Effects of Trust in Leadership on Employee Performance, Behavior, and Attitudes: A Meta-Analysis," paper presented at the Academy of Management Conference, Toronto, Canada, August 2000; and K.T. Dirks, "Trust in Leadership and Team Performance: Evidence from NCAA Basketball," *Journal of Applied Psychology*, December 2000, pp. 1004–12.

26. Based on F.E. Fiedler, "Leadership Experience and Leadership Performance: Another Hypothesis Shot to Hell," *Organizational Behavior and Human Performance*, January 1970, pp. 1–14; F.E. Fiedler, "Time-Based Measures of Leadership Experience and Organizational Performance: A Review of Research and a Preliminary Model," *Leadership Quarterly*, Spring 1992, pp. 5–23; and M.A. Quinones, J.K. Ford, and M.S. Teachout, "The Relationship Between Work Experience and Job Performance: A Conceptual and Meta-Analytic Review," *Personnel Psychology*, Winter 1995, pp. 887–910.

27. Based on R.G. Lord, C.L. DeVader, and G.M. Alliger, "A Meta-Analysis of the Relation Between Personality Traits and Leadership Perceptions: An Application of Validity Generalization Procedures," *Journal of Applied Psychology*, August 1986, pp. 402–10; J.R. Meindl, S.B. Ehrlich, and J.M. Dukerich, "The Romance of Leadership," *Administrative Science Quarterly*, March 1985, pp. 78–102; and B.M. Staw and J. Ross, "Commitment in an Experimenting Society: A Study of the Attribution of Leadership from Administrative Scenerios," *Journal of Applied Psychology*, June 1980, pp. 249–60.

The Truth About Managing People . . . and Nothing but the Truth

28. Based on R.M. Entman, "Framing: Toward Clarification of a Fractured Paradigm," *Journal of Communication*, Autumn 1993, pp. 51–58; G.T. Fairhurst and R.A. Sarr, *The Art of Framing: Managing the Language of Leadership* (San Francisco: Jossey-Bass, 1996); and R.S. Dunham, "When Is a Tax Cut Not a Tax Cut?," *Business Week*, March 19, 2001, pp. 38–39.

29. Based on D. Eden and A.B. Shani, "Pygmalion Goes to Boot Camp: Expectancy, Leadership, and Trainee Performance," *Journal of Applied Psychology*, April 1982, pp. 194–99; and D. Eden, "Leadership and Expectations: Pygmalion Effects and Other Self-Fulfilling Prophecies in Organizations," *Leadership Quarterly*, Winter 1992, pp. 271–305.

30. Based on R.E. Kelley, "In Praise of Followers," *Harvard Business Review*, November–December 1988, pp. 142–48; and I. Chaleff, *The Courageous Follower: Standing Up To and For Our Leaders* (San Francisco: Berrett-Koehler, 1995).

31. Based on J.A. Conger and R.N. Kanungo (eds.), *Charismatic Leadership in Organizations* (Thousand Oaks, CA: Sage, 1998); and J.M. Howell and P.J. Frost, "A Laboratory Study of Charismatic Leadership," *Organizational Behavior and Human Decision Processes*, April 1989, pp. 243–69.

32. Based on R.E. Emerson, "Power-Dependence Relations," *American Sociological Review*, vol. 27 (1962), pp. 31–41; and H. Mintzberg, *Power In and Around Organizations* (Upper Saddle River, NJ: Prentice Hall, 1983).

33. Based on R.J. House, "Path-Goal Theory of Leadership: Lessons, Legacy, and a Reformulation," *Leadership Quarterly*, Fall 1996, pp. 323–52.

34. Based on "Military-Style Management in China," *Asia Inc.*, March 1995, p. 70; and M.F. Peterson and J.G. Hunt, "International Perspectives on International Leadership," *Leadership Quarterly*, Fall 1997, pp. 203–31.

35. Based on S. Kerr and J.M. Jermier, "Substitutes for Leadership: Their Meaning and Measurement," *Organizational Behavior and Human Performance*, December 1978, pp. 375–403; and cites in J. Useem, "Conquering Vertical Limits," *Fortune*, February 19, 2001, p. 94.

36. Based on S.P. Robbins and P.L. Hunsaker, *Training in InterPersonal Skills: TIPS for Managing People at Work*, 2nd ed. (Upper Saddle River, NJ: Prentice Hall, 1996), pp. 34–39.

37. Based on R.L. Daft and R.H. Lengel, "Information Richness: A New Approach to Managerial Behavior and Organization Design," in B.M. Staw and L.L. Cummings (eds.), *Research in Organizational Behavior*, vol. 6 (Greenwich, CT: JAI Press, 1984), pp. 191–233; and E. Wong, "A Stinging Office Memo Boomerangs," *New York Times*, April 5, 2001, p. C1.

38. Based on R.L. Rosnow and G.A. Fine, *Rumor and Gossip: The Social Psychology of Hearsay* (New York: Elsevier, 1976); L. Hirschhorn, "Managing Rumors," in L. Hirschhorn (ed.), *Cutting Back* (San Francisco: Jossey-Bass, 1983); M. Noon and R. Delbridge, "News from Behind My Hand: Gossip in Organizations," *Organization Studies*, 14, no. 1 (1993), pp. 23–36; and B. McKay, "At Coke, Layoffs Inspire All Manner of Peculiar Rumors," *Wall Street Journal*, October 17, 2000, p. A1.

39. Based on D. Tannen, *You Just Don't Understand: Women and Men in Conversation* (New York: Ballentine Books, 1991); and D. Tannen, *Talking from 9 to 5* (New York: William Morrow, 1995).

40. Based on A. Bandura, *Social Learning Theory* (Upper Saddle River, NJ: Prentice Hall, 1977).

41. Based on J. P. Schuster, J. Carpenter, and M.P. Kane, *The Power of Open-Book Management* (New York: John Wiley, 1996); and T.R.V. Davis, "Open-Book Management: Its Promise and Pitfalls," *Organizational Dynamics*, Winter 1997, pp. 7–20.

42. Based on M.A. Campion, E.M. Papper, and G.J. Medsker, "Relations Between Work Team Characteristics and Effectiveness: A Replication and Extension," *Personnel Psychology*, Summer 1996, pp. 429–52; D.E. Hyatt and T.M. Ruddy, "An Examination of the Relationship Between Work Group Characteristics and Performance: Once More Into the Breach," *Personnel Psychology*, Autumn 1997, pp. 553–85; S.G. Cohen and D.E. Bailey, "What Makes Teams Work: Group Effectiveness Research from the Shop Floor to the Executive Suite," *Journal of Management*, vol. 23, no. 3 (1997), pp. 239–90; A.D. Shulman, "Putting Group Information Technology in its Place: Communication and Good Work Group Performance," in S.R. Clegg, C. Hardy, and W.R. Nord (eds.), *Managing Organizations: Current Issues* (London: Sage, 1999), pp. 107–21; G.A. Neuman and J. Wright, "Team Effectiveness: Beyond Skills and Cognitive Ability," *Journal of Applied Psychology*, June 1999, pp. 376–89; P.J. Hinds, K.M. Carley, D. Krackhardt, and D. Wholey, "Choosing Work Group Members: Balancing Similarity, Competence, and Familiarity," *Organizational Behavior and Human Decision Processes*, March 2000, pp. 226–51; and G.L. Stewart and M.R. Barrick, "Team Structure and Performance: Assessing the Mediating Role of Intrateam Process and the Moderating Role of Task Type," *Academy of Management Journal*, April 2000, pp. 135–48.

43. Based on S.J. Karau and K.D. Williams, "Social Loafing: A Meta-Analytic Review and Theoretical Integration," *Journal of Personality and Social Psychology*, October 1993, pp. 681–706; and D.R. Comer, "A Model of Social Loafing in Real Work Groups," *Human Relations*, June 1995, pp. 647–67.

44. Based on J. Greenberg, "Equity and Workplace Status: A Field Experiment," *Journal of Applied Psychology*, November 1988, pp. 606–13; and B. Headlam, "How to E-Mail Like a C.E.O.," *New York Times Magazine*, April 8, 2001, pp. 7–8.

45. Based on A. Sinclair, "The Tyranny of a Team Ideology," *Organization Studies*, vol. 13, no. 4 (1992), pp. 611–26; and J. Prieto, "The Team Perspective in Selection and Assessment," in H. Schuler, J.L. Farr, and M. Smith (eds.), *Personnel Selection and Assessment: Industrial and Organizational Perspectives* (Hillsdale, NJ: Erlbaum, 1994).

46. Based on S.P. Robbins, *Managing Organizational Conflict: A Nontraditional Approach* (Upper Saddle River, NJ: Prentice Hall, 1974); K.A. Jehn, "A Qualitative Analysis of Conflict Types and Dimensions in Organizational Groups," *Administrative Science Quarterly*, September 1997, pp. 530–57; C.J. Nemeth, J.B. Connell, J.D. Rogers, and K.S. Brown, "Improving Decision Making by Means of Dissent," *Journal of Applied Social Psychology*, January 2001, pp. 48–58; and K.A. Jehn and E.A. Mannix, "The Dynamic Nature of Conflict: A Longitudinal Study of Intragroup Conflict and Group Performance," *Academy of Management Journal*, April 2001, pp. 238–51.

47. Based on S.P. Robbins, *Managing Organizational Conflict: A Nontraditional Approach* (Upper Saddle River, NJ: Prentice Hall, 1974).

48. Based on I.L. Janis, *Groupthink: Psychological Studies of Policy Decisions and Fiascoes*, 2nd ed. (Boston: Houghton Mifflin, 1982); W. Park, "A Review of Research on Groupthink," *Journal of Behavioral Decision Making*, July 1990, pp. 229–45; and G. Moorhead, R. Ference, and C.P. Neck, "Group Decision Fiascos Continue: Space Shuttle Challenger and a Revised Groupthink Framework," *Human Relations*, May 1991, pp. 539–50.

49. Based on P. Cappelli, J. Constantine, and C. Chadwick, "It Pays to Value Family: Work and Family Tradeoffs Reconsidered," *Industrial Relations*, April 2000, pp. 175–98; M.A. Verespej, "Balancing Act," *Industry Week*, May 15, 2000, pp. 81–85; J. Lardner, "World-Class Workaholics," *U.S. News & World Report*, December 20, 1999, p. 42; M. Conlin, "9 to 5 Isn't Working Anymore," *Business Week*,

September 20, 1999, p. 94; "The New World of Work: Flexibility Is the Watchword," *Business Week*, January 10, 2000, p. 36; S. Shellenbarger, "What Job Candidates Really Want to Know: Will I Have a Life?," *Wall Street Journal*, November 17, 1999, p. B1; P–W. Tam, "Silicon Valley Belatedly Boots Up Programs to Ease Employees' Lives," *Wall Street Journal*, August 29, 2000, p. B1; C. Oglesby, "More Options for Moms Seeking Work-Family Balance," *cnn.com*, May 10, 2001; and R.C. Barnett and D.T. Hall, "How to Use Reduced Hours to Win the War for Talent," *Organizational Dynamics*, vol. 29, no. 3, 2001, pp. 192–210.

50. Based on G.R. Salancik and J. Pfeffer, "A Social Information Processing Approach to Job Attitudes and Task Design," *Administrative Science Quarterly*, June 1978, pp. 224–53; and J.G. Thomas and R.W. Griffin, "The Power of Social Information in the Workplace," *Organizational Dynamics*, Autumn 1989, pp. 63–75.

51. Based on J.P. Wanous, "Individual Differences and Reactions to Job Characteristics," *Journal of Applied Psychology*, October 1974, pp. 616–22; and H.P. Sims and A.D. Szilagyi, "Job Characteristic Relationships: Individual and Structural Moderators," *Organizational Behavior and Human Performance*, June 1976, pp. 211–30.

52. Based on J.R. Hackman, "Work Design," in J.R. Hackman and J.L. Suttle (eds.), *Improving Life at Work* (Santa Monica, CA: Goodyear, 1977), pp. 132–33.

53. Based on R.J. Burke, "Why Performance Appraisal Systems Fail," *Personnel Administration*, June 1972, pp. 32–40; and H.H. Meyer, "A Solution to the Performance Appraisal Feedback Enigma," *Academy of Management Executive*, February 1991, pp. 68–76.

54. Based on H.H. Kelley, "Attribution in Social Interaction," in E. Jones et al (eds.), *Attribution: Perceiving the Causes of Behavior* (Morristown, NJ: General Learning Press, 1972).

55. Based on W.W. Tornow and M. London (eds.), *Maximizing the Value of 360-Degree Feedback* (San Francsico: Jossey-Bass, 1998); L.E. Atwater, C. Ostroff, F.J. Yammarino, and J.W. Fleenor, "Self-Other Agreement: Does It Really Matter?" *Personnel Psychology*, Autumn 1998, pp. 577–98; G.J. Greguras and C. Robie, "A New Look at Within-Source Interrater Reliability of 360-Degree Feedback Ratings," *Journal of Applied Psychology*, December 1998, pp. 960–68; and J.D. Facteau and S.B. Craig, "Are Performance Ratings From Different Rating Sources Compatible?" *Journal of Applied Psychology*, April 2001, pp. 215–27.

56. Based on D.A. Nadler, "The Effective Management of Organizational Change," in J.W. Lorsch (ed.), *Handbook of Organizational Behavior* (Upper Saddle River, NJ: Prentice Hall, 1987), pp. 358–69; and P. Stebel, "Why Do Employees Resist Change?," *Harvard Business Review*, May–June 1996, pp. 86–92.

57. Based on D.R. Davies, G. Matthews, and C.S.K. Wong, "Ageing and Work," in C.L. Cooper and I.T. Robertson (eds.), *International Review of Industrial and Organizational Psychology*, vol. 6 (Chichester, England: Wiley, 1991), pp. 159–65.

58. Based on J.P. Kotter and L.A. Schlesinger, "Choosing Strategies for Change," *Harvard Business Review*, March–April 1979, pp. 106–14; and J.L. Cotton, *Employee Involvement* (Newbury Park, CA: Sage, 1993).

59. Based on D.M. Noer, *Healing the Wounds* (San Francisco, CA: Jossey-Bass, 1993); and S.P. Robbins, "Layoff-Survivor Sickness: A Missing Topic in Organizational Behavior," *Journal of Management Education*, February 1999, pp. 31–43.

60. Based on C.A. Kiesler, R.E. Nisbett, and M.P. Zanna, "On Inferring One's Belief from One's Behavior," *Journal of Personality and Social Psychology*, April 1969, pp. 321–27; and D.J. Bem, "Self-Perception Theory," in L. Berkowitz (ed.), *Advances in Experimental Social Psychology*, vol. 6 (New York: Academic Press, 1972), pp. 1–62.

61. Based on M. London and M.D. Hakel, "Effects of Applicant Stereotypes, Order, and Information on Interview Impressions," *Journal of Applied Psychology*, April 1974, pp. 157–62; N.R. Bardack and F.T. McAndrew, "The Influence of Physical Attractiveness and Manner of Dress on Success in a Simulated Personnel Decision," *Journal of Social Psychology*, August 1985, pp. 777–78; and T.M. Macan and R.L. Dipboye, "The Relationship of the Interviewers' Preinterview Impressions to Selection and Recruitment Outcomes," *Personnel Psychology*, Autumn 1990, pp. 745–69.

62. Based on S. Fineman (ed.), *Emotion in Organizations*, 2nd ed. (Thousand Oaks, CA: Sage, 2000); B.E. Ashforth and R.H. Humphrey, "Emotion in the Workplace: A Reappraisal," *Human Relations*, February 1995, pp. 97–125; N.M. Ashkanasy, C.E.J. Hartel, and W.J. Zerbe (eds.), *Emotions in the Workplace: Research, Theory, and Practice* (Westport, CT: Quorum Books, 2000); and R. Bar-On and J.D.A. Parker (eds.), *The Handbook of Emotional Intelligence: Theory, Development, Assessment, and Application at Home, School, and in the Workplace* (San Francisco: Jossey-Bass, 2000).

63. Based on M.E. McGill, *American Business and Quick Fix* (New York: Henry Holt, 1988); and B.M. Staw and L.D. Epstein, "What Bandwagons Bring: Effects of Popular Management Techniques on Corporate Performance, Reputation, and CEO Pay," *Administrative Science Quarterly*, September 2000, pp. 523–56.

The *Financial Times* delivers a world of business news.

Use the Risk-Free Trial Voucher below!

To stay ahead in today's business world you need to be well-informed on a daily basis. And not just on the national level. You need a news source that closely monitors the entire world of business, and then delivers it in a concise, quick-read format.

With the *Financial Times* you get the major stories from every region of the world. Reports found nowhere else. You get business, management, politics, economics, technology and more.

Now you can try the *Financial Times* for 4 weeks, absolutely risk free. And better yet, if you wish to continue receiving the *Financial Times* you'll get great savings off the regular subscription rate. Just use the voucher below.

4 Week Risk-Free Trial Voucher

Yes! Please send me the *Financial Times* for 4 weeks (Monday through Saturday) Risk-Free, and details of special subscription rates in my country.

Name_____

Company_____

Address _____ ❏ Business or   ❏ Home Address

Apt./Suite/Floor _____City _____State/Province_____

Zip/Postal Code_____Country _____

Phone (optional) _____E-mail (optional)_____

Limited time offer good for new subscribers in FT delivery areas only.

To order contact Financial Times Customer Service in your area (mention offer SAB01A).

The Americas: Tel 800-628-8088 Fax 845-566-8220 E-mail: uscirculation@ft.com

Europe: Tel 44 20 7873 4200 Fax 44 20 7873 3428 E-mail: fte.subs@ft.com

Japan: Tel 0120 341-468 Fax 0120 593-146 E-mail: circulation.fttokyo@ft.com

Korea: E-mail: sungho.yang@ft.com

S.E. Asia: Tel 852 2905 5555 Fax 852 2905 5590 E-mail: subseasia@ft.com

www.ft.com

FT FINANCIAL TIMES
World business newspaper

8 reasons why you should read the Financial Times for 4 weeks RISK-FREE!

To help you stay current with significant developments in the world economy ...
and to assist you to make informed business decisions — the Financial Times brings you:

① Fast, meaningful overviews of international affairs ... plus daily briefings on major world news.

② Perceptive coverage of economic, business, financial and political developments with special focus on emerging markets.

③ More international business news than any other publication.

④ Sophisticated financial analysis and commentary on world market activity plus stock quotes from over 30 countries.

⑤ Reports on international companies and a section on global investing.

⑥ Specialized pages on management, marketing, advertising and technological innovations from all parts of the world.

⑦ Highly valued single-topic special reports (over 200 annually) on countries, industries, investment opportunities, technology and more.

⑧ The Saturday Weekend FT section — a globetrotter's guide to leisure-time activities around the world: the arts, fine dining, travel, sports and more.

For Special Offer See Over

FT FINANCIAL TIMES
World business newspaper

Where to find tomorrow's best business and technology ideas. TODAY.

- Ideas for defining tomorrow's competitive strategies — and executing them.

- Ideas that reflect a profound understanding of today's global business realities.

- Ideas that will help you achieve unprecedented customer and enterprise value.

- Ideas that illuminate the powerful new connections between business and technology.

ONE PUBLISHER.
Financial Times Prentice Hall.

FINANCIAL TIMES
Prentice Hall

WORLD BUSINESS PUBLISHER

AND 3 GREAT WEB SITES:

ft-ph.com

Fast access to all Financial Times Prentice Hall business books currently available.

InformIt.com

Your link to today's top business and technology experts: new content, practical solutions, and the world's best online training.

Business-minds.com

Where the thought leaders of the business world gather to share key ideas, techniques, resources — and inspiration.